I0704346

ANXIOUS

ATTACHMENT

RECOVERY:

From Clingy to Confident:

A Practical Guide to Build Secure, Loving Relationships and Overcome Fear of Rejection and Abandonment in 12 Weeks

Copyright © 2024 by Ruth D. Smith

All rights reserved. No part of this publication may be reproduced, distributed, or transmitted in any form or by any means, including photocopying, recording, or other electronic or mechanical methods, without the prior written permission of the publisher, except in the case of brief quotations embodied in critical reviews and certain other non-commercial uses permitted by copyright law. For permission requests, please contact the publisher at the address below.

Disclaimer

This book is intended for informational and educational purposes only and is not a substitute for professional mental health care, therapy, counseling, or other medical advice. The strategies, tools, and insights shared are based on research and personal experience but are not meant to diagnose, treat, or cure any specific mental health condition.

Do not disregard or delay seeking professional advice because of something you have read in this book. The author and publisher are not liable for any actions taken as a result of reading this book.

Note: Individual experiences and results may vary.

TABLE OF CONTENTS

INTRODUCTION 1

Your attachment recovery journey begins here 1

Why Anxious Attachment Affects Relationships 4

Understanding the 12-Week Roadmap 8

What Is Anxious Attachment and Why Does It Matter? 14

Introduction to Cognitive-Behavioral Techniques for Attachment

Recovery 16

PART 1: UNDERSTANDING YOUR ATTACHMENT STYLE 20

CHAPTER 1: THE SCIENCE OF ATTACHMENT: HOW IT SHAPES YOUR RELATIONSHIPS 21

Attachment Theories 21

Different Attachment Styles 23

How Early Relationships Shape Adult Attachment Styles 26

CHAPTER 2: IDENTIFYING YOUR ATTACHMENT STYLE 29

Self-assessment quiz 29

Red Flags in Relationships 34

Attachment Behaviors 38

CHAPTER 3: ATTACHMENT STYLES IN ACTION 43

Real-Life Examples 43

The Emotional Rollercoaster 46

Observe Attachment Styles 49

PART 2: OVERCOMING FEAR OF REJECTION AND ABANDONMENT 54

CHAPTER 4: BREAKING FREE FROM FEAR OF ABANDONMENT 55

The Fear Cycle.. 56

How Fear Drives Emotions... 58

The Subtle Signs of Fear-Based Actions 62

CHAPTER 5: MANAGING ANXIETY IN RELATIONSHIPS........................... 65

Tools for Reducing Anxiety.. 65

Techniques to Halt Negative Spirals 68

Emotion Regulation Strategies.. 71

CHAPTER 6: HEALING THE INNER CHILD 75

Unresolved Emotional Wounds.. 76

Practical Exercises to Soothe and Heal Your Inner Child 79

PART 3: BUILDING CONFIDENCE AND EMOTIONAL SECURITY 84

CHAPTER 7: REWIRING YOUR ATTACHMENT PATTERNS 85

From Anxious to Secure Attachment.................................. 85

ExercisesTop of Form 88

Shifting from Fear-Driven Reactions to Calm, Confident Responses....... 91

CHAPTER 8: BUILDING SELF-WORTH AND INNER CONFIDENCE........... 97

Secure Sense of Self... 97

Detaching Your Self-Worth from Outcomes 100

Mindfulness Practices... 103

CHAPTER 9: SETTING HEALTHY BOUNDARIES 107

The Importance of Boundaries.. 107

How to assert your needs... 109

Setting limits without fear... 112

PART 4: FOSTERING SECURE AND LOVING RELATIONSHIPS.................116

CHAPTER 10: BUILDING TRUST AND EMOTIONAL INTIMACY 117

WHY IT MATTERS.. 117

EMOTIONAL INTIMACY 121

DEEPENING CONNECTION 125

CHAPTER 11: COMMUNICATING IN SECURE RELATIONSHIPS 131

COMMUNICATE WITHOUT FEAR 131

CONFLICT RESOLUTION 135

POWER OF VULNERABILITY 139

CHAPTER 12: CREATING A SECURE LOVE FOUNDATION 143

CREATE AND SUSTAIN LOVE 143

REINFORCING EMOTIONAL SECURITY 146

WHEN SETBACKS OCCUR?.. 149

PART 5: YOUR 12-WEEK JOURNEY TO SECURE ATTACHMENT............154

CHAPTER 13: WEEK-BY-WEEK ACTION PLAN 155

WEEKLY CHALLENGES... 159

CHAPTER 14: MAINTAINING YOUR EMOTIONAL GROWTH 187

HOW TO STAY ON THE PATH... 187

BUILDING SUPPORT SYSTEMS... 190

COGNITIVE-BEHAVIORAL TOOLS... 193

CONCLUSION 197

LIVE CONFIDENTLY AND SECURELY....................................... 200

INTRODUCTION

Your attachment recovery journey begins here

Hey there! I'm so glad you've picked up this book because it means you're ready to take the first step towards building the kind of relationships you deserve—secure, loving, and fulfilling. If you're like many people who struggle with anxious attachment, I imagine you've felt a lot of emotional highs and lows in your relationships. Maybe you've worried about being left or feared that you're not enough for your partner. I get it, and I want you to know that you're not alone in feeling this way.

The good news? Change is possible. Whether you've been stuck in a cycle of fear and insecurity for years or just started to realize your attachment style is causing problems, this book is your roadmap to recovery.

What to Expect from This Book

This isn't just a book filled with theories. While understanding why we behave the way we do is important (and we'll get to that), this book is all about practical steps. Each chapter will guide you through exercises and techniques specifically designed to help you break free from anxiety-driven patterns, gain emotional stability, and start experiencing the kind of relationships where you feel safe, secure, and loved.

We're going to take this one step at a time over the course of 12 weeks. By the end, you'll have the tools you need to go from feeling clingy and insecure to confident and grounded. And guess what? You don't have to wait until the end to start feeling better. As we move through each chapter, you'll notice gradual changes that make you feel more secure in your relationships—both with others and, most importantly, with yourself.

The Structure of the Book: Your 12-Week Roadmap
Here's how we'll tackle this journey together:

Understanding Your Attachment Style: First, we'll help you understand your attachment style and why it matters so much in relationships. We'll explore what anxious attachment looks like, how it develops, and how it might be affecting you today. You'll also learn how to recognize it in yourself and your behaviors. This is where you'll get the foundation you need to start making meaningful changes.

Overcoming Fear and Anxiety: Next, we'll dive into the root of anxious attachment—fear of rejection and abandonment. We'll explore what drives this fear and, more importantly, how to manage and overcome it. You'll get practical tools to quiet those anxious thoughts and feelings that make you doubt yourself or your partner.

Building Confidence and Emotional Security: Once we've tackled your fears, we'll focus on helping you build up your confidence. You'll learn how to shift from feeling needy or clingy to secure and confident. We'll work on setting healthy boundaries, boosting your self-worth, and cultivating emotional resilience so that you can approach relationships from a place of strength, not fear.

Fostering Secure and Loving Relationships: Finally, we'll look at how to create and maintain secure, lasting relationships. You'll learn how to build trust, communicate better, and foster deep emotional intimacy. By the end, you'll have the tools to create the kind of relationship where both you and your partner feel secure, understood, and valued.

What You'll Achieve by the End

By following this step-by-step approach, you'll be able to:

- Recognize and understand your anxious attachment patterns.
- Manage your fear of rejection and abandonment in healthier ways.

- Build emotional security, both within yourself and in your relationships.

- Feel more confident, secure, and self-assured when it comes to love.

- Foster deep, meaningful, and stable connections with others.

This book is your guide, but the real work—and the real reward—comes from within you. You've already taken a huge step by being here. Now, let's start the journey to becoming the most secure and confident version of yourself.

Are you ready? Let's get started!

Why Anxious Attachment Affects Relationships

Let's take a moment to talk about why anxious attachment can make relationships so challenging. If you're someone who struggles with this attachment style, you might have noticed patterns in how you interact with your partner—patterns that leave you feeling anxious, insecure, or even desperate for reassurance. These feelings aren't random. They stem from a deep-rooted fear of rejection or abandonment, and they can cast a shadow over even the most loving relationships.

The Fear That Won't Go Away

If you've ever caught yourself thinking, *"What if they leave me?"* or *"Do they really love me?"*—even in a secure relationship—you're not alone. Anxious attachment makes us hyper-aware of any potential signs of rejection, real or imagined. You might find yourself overanalyzing your partner's every move or seeking constant validation just to feel secure. The problem is, that need for reassurance can sometimes push your partner away, creating the very thing you fear the most.

It's a vicious cycle: the more anxious you feel, the more you seek reassurance, but the more you seek reassurance, the more your partner may pull back. And when they do, that only confirms your worst fears. Sound familiar?

Where Does This Come From?

Anxious attachment usually develops in childhood. If you grew up with caregivers who were inconsistent—sometimes loving, but other times emotionally distant—you may have learned that love isn't something you can fully count on. You might have felt like you had to "earn" affection or work hard to keep people close. Now, as an adult, those feelings can carry over into your romantic relationships, making it hard to trust that love will stay.

But here's the thing: these feelings, while strong, aren't facts. They're based on old patterns that your mind is used to repeating. The good news? With some awareness and effort, you can rewire the way you approach relationships.

How It Plays Out in Relationships

When you're anxious about being left or rejected, it's easy to fall into habits that hurt your relationships. You might:

- **Cling too tightly:** You hold on for dear life because you're afraid of losing the person. But this can feel suffocating for your partner, making them pull back, which only fuels your anxiety.
- **Overthink everything:** You read too much into small things—like a delayed text or a change in your partner's tone—assuming the worst. This overthinking drains your emotional energy and often leads to unnecessary conflict.
- **Put your partner on a pedestal:** You might prioritize their needs and feelings so much that you forget about your own, hoping that if you're perfect enough, they'll never leave.
- **Avoid addressing your own needs**: Sometimes, you're so focused on keeping the peace and holding onto the relationship that you neglect what you truly want or need. Over time, this creates resentment and frustration.

None of this is your fault. These behaviors stem from a desire to feel safe and loved, but ironically, they often sabotage the very closeness you crave.

The Impact on You and Your Partner

When you're constantly in a state of anxiety, it's exhausting—for you and your partner. You may feel like you're on an emotional rollercoaster, where one day you're feeling loved and secure, and the next, you're questioning everything. This takes a toll not only on your mental health but also on the health of your relationship.

Your partner, on the other hand, might start to feel overwhelmed by the pressure to constantly reassure you. They might pull away, not because they don't care, but because they're unsure of how to navigate your emotional needs. This can lead to misunderstandings, conflicts, and a growing emotional distance.

But here's the thing: this *doesn't* have to be your relationship story forever. Understanding these patterns is the first step toward breaking them. And throughout this book, we're going to dive into how you can shift away from anxious attachment and toward a more secure, balanced, and fulfilling connection with both you and your partner.

A New Way Forward

Anxious attachment might be a part of your life right now, but it doesn't define you. With the right tools, you can move beyond fear and insecurity and start building relationships that feel safe, stable, and genuinely loving.

Remember, you deserve to feel secure in your relationships, and the journey to that starts right here, right now. Let's walk this path together—toward the kind of love that feels strong, steady, and full of trust.

Understanding the 12-Week Roadmap

Over the next 12 weeks, we're going to walk through a carefully structured roadmap that's designed to give you practical tools, insights, and exercises. The goal? To help you shift from anxious attachment and relationship anxiety to emotional resilience and security. By the end of this journey, you'll have the tools to foster a healthier, more balanced relationship with yourself—and others.

Let's break down what this roadmap looks like, so you know exactly where you're headed.

Week 1-2: Laying the Foundation – Understanding Your Attachment Style

We start by getting to the heart of anxious attachment. Before we dive into change, it's important to understand where these patterns come from and how they show up in your life. During these first two weeks, we'll focus on:

- **Self-reflection:** You'll explore your attachment history and how your past relationships have shaped your current ones.
- **Identifying triggers:** We'll work together to pinpoint the exact moments that activate your anxiety in relationships, so you can start gaining control over them.
- **Building awareness:** By understanding your anxious tendencies, you'll develop a foundation for change. This will help you see your patterns with clarity, which is the first step toward transforming them.

Week 3-4: Rewriting Your Story – Challenging Negative Thought Patterns

By now, you'll have a clearer sense of your emotional triggers and how anxious attachment has impacted your relationships. Weeks 3 and 4 are about challenging the negative thoughts and beliefs that fuel your anxiety. Here, we'll focus on:

- **Cognitive restructuring:** You'll learn how to identify and reframe the automatic negative thoughts that make you feel insecure and unloved.

- **Interrupting overthinking:** Anxious attachment thrives on overanalyzing situations. We'll dive into techniques that help you break free from the cycle of overthinking, so you can focus on what's real, rather than what's imagined.

- **Practicing self-compassion**: You'll start building a kinder, more supportive inner dialogue, which is essential for moving toward emotional resilience.

Week 5-6: Shifting Your Focus – Building Emotional Security

Now that you've started to challenge the old thought patterns, it's time to shift your focus. In weeks 5 and 6, we'll move from anxious reactivity to creating a sense of emotional security within yourself. This part is all about:

- **Developing self-soothing techniques:** You'll learn practical methods to calm your anxiety in the moment, so you don't feel dependent on external reassurance.

- **Strengthening self-awareness:** You'll explore how to listen to your emotions and respond to them in healthy, constructive ways, rather than feeling overwhelmed or reactive.

- **Building trust with yourself**: This is a key step in breaking free from anxious attachment. By learning to trust your own instincts and emotional resilience, you'll reduce the need for constant validation from others.

Week 7-8: Creating Secure Relationships – Communication and Boundaries

Now that you've strengthened your relationship with yourself, we'll turn our attention to building healthier connections with others. In weeks 7 and 8, we'll focus on:

- **Effective communication:** You'll learn how to express your needs in a way that fosters connection, rather than creating conflict or distance.

- **Setting healthy boundaries:** This is a big one for anxious attachers. We'll work on how to set and maintain boundaries that respect both your needs and your partner's, without feeling guilty or fearful of rejection.

- **Practicing vulnerability:** You'll explore how to open emotionally without feeling like you're putting yourself at risk. Vulnerability, when done right, builds stronger, more secure relationships.

Week 9-10: Rebuilding Trust – With Yourself and Your Partner

Trust is a key ingredient in secure relationships, but when you have anxious attachment, trusting both yourself and others can feel difficult. In weeks 9 and 10, we'll dive into:

- **Rebuilding self-trust:** You'll continue to develop a stronger connection with your inner self, so that you can rely on your own emotional strength, rather than looking outward for validation.
- **Fostering trust in your relationship:** You'll learn strategies for building (or rebuilding) trust with your partner, focusing on open communication, consistency, and emotional safety.
- **Letting go of fear:** Fear of abandonment can keep you stuck in unhealthy patterns. We'll work on releasing that fear and replacing it with confidence in your ability to navigate relationships.

Week 11-12: Cultivating Long-Term Emotional Resilience

By the final two weeks, you'll have a toolkit of strategies for managing your emotions and fostering secure relationships. These weeks are all about setting yourself up for long-term success. Here's what we'll cover:

- **Strengthening your new habits:** You'll focus on integrating everything you've learned, so these changes become second nature.

- **Preparing for challenges:** Life and relationships are never perfect. We'll talk about how to handle setbacks or difficult moments without slipping back into anxious patterns.

- **Celebrating your progress:** Finally, you'll take time to acknowledge how far you've come. Emotional resilience is a journey, and you deserve to celebrate each step you've taken toward creating more secure, loving relationships.

Why This Roadmap Works

This 12-week roadmap isn't about quick fixes or surface-level changes. It's designed to give you a step-by-step guide to transform how you approach relationships from the inside out. By understanding your attachment style, challenging your old beliefs, and developing practical tools, you'll be able to cultivate emotional resilience that lasts far beyond the 12 weeks.

Each week builds on the last, ensuring that you're making sustainable progress toward feeling more confident, secure, and in control of your emotional world. And remember, I'm with you every step of the way.

What Is Anxious Attachment and Why Does It Matter?

Now that we've laid out your 12-week roadmap, let's take a moment to dive deeper into what we mean by "anxious attachment." Understanding this is essential, because it explains so much about why you may be feeling the way you do in your relationships. And trust me, you're not alone in this—far from it.

Defining Anxious Attachment

Anxious attachment is a relationship pattern that often forms early in life. It's how we learned to connect with others when we were kids, particularly with our caregivers. If those early experiences involved inconsistent care—sometimes loving, sometimes unavailable—we may have developed a deep-seated fear of abandonment. As adults, this fear can show up as an intense need for reassurance, validation, and closeness in relationships.

You might feel a strong emotional pull to be close to your partner, but at the same time, you're worried they'll leave or that you're not enough for them. You may find yourself overthinking small interactions, questioning your worth, or feeling jealous and insecure—especially when things get a little shaky.

Sound familiar? That's anxious attachment at work. It's not just a "quirk" of your personality. It's a survival mechanism you learned to protect yourself from getting hurt. But here's the catch: what once helped you feel safe is now getting in the way of you feeling secure in your relationships.

How Anxious Attachment Impacts Your Relationship Patterns and Self-Esteem

If you have anxious attachment, you probably find yourself feeling like you're on an emotional rollercoaster in your relationships. When things are good, you feel amazing—almost euphoric—but the second there's a hint of distance or uncertainty, panic sets in. You may become hyper-focused on your partner's every word and action, looking for signs that something's wrong, even when nothing's happened.

This can make your relationships feel exhausting, both for you and your partner. You might find yourself:

- **Needing constant reassurance:** Asking your partner if they still love you, if they're upset, or if they're going to leave— even if there's no reason to think they will.

- **Overanalyzing conversations:** Going over texts or things they said, wondering if there's a hidden meaning or if you somehow messed up.

- **Fearing rejection:** The smallest signs of distance or a change in behavior can feel like a threat, triggering intense feelings of insecurity or even panic.

Feeling "too much" or "not enough": These opposing feelings can leave you feeling confused and stuck, as if you're always trying to prove your worth or hold onto your partner's affection.

Over time, these patterns take a toll on your self-esteem. It's hard to feel good about yourself when you're constantly doubting your value or worrying that the people you love most are going to leave. And the truth is, these feelings often create the very problems you're trying to avoid.

But—and this is a big but—this is where real change can happen. Once you understand what's happening and why, you can start breaking free from the patterns that are holding you back.

Introduction to Cognitive-Behavioral Techniques for Attachment Recovery

Here's the good news: you don't have to stay stuck in anxious attachment forever. One of the most effective ways to heal is by using cognitive-behavioral techniques (CBT). CBT is a proven approach that helps you understand the connection between your thoughts, emotions, and behaviors—and how you can change them to create healthier, more secure relationships.

We'll be using these techniques throughout the book to help you:

- **Identify unhelpful thought patterns:** The anxious stories you tell yourself, like "I'm not good enough" or "They'll leave me," can be rewritten. CBT will help you catch these thoughts and challenge them, so they don't control your emotions and actions.

- **Change reactive behaviors:** Whether it's texting your partner repeatedly for reassurance or withdrawing emotionally out of fear, CBT will guide you in recognizing these habits and replacing them with healthier responses.

- **Build self-trust and confidence:** The more you learn to manage your thoughts and feelings, the more you'll trust yourself to handle whatever comes your way. This is a key step in breaking free from anxious attachment and moving toward emotional security.

Throughout the book, I'll be walking you through specific exercises designed to help you apply these techniques in your everyday life. With each step, you'll get closer to feeling more confident, more secure, and more at ease in your relationships.

You've already shown incredible strength by seeking answers and taking steps toward change. Remember, anxious attachment doesn't define you—it's just one part of your story, and together, we're going to rewrite it.

Let's dive into this journey of recovery, so you can build the secure, loving relationships you deserve.

PART 1: UNDERSTANDING YOUR ATTACHMENT STYLE

CHAPTER 1: THE SCIENCE OF ATTACHMENT: HOW IT SHAPES YOUR RELATIONSHIPS

Attachment Theories

Let's start at the beginning, with the origins of attachment theory—because understanding where these ideas come from can help you make sense of your own experiences.

Attachment theory was developed in the mid-20th century by psychologist John Bowlby. He was curious about why some children clung to their caregivers more than others, while some seemed indifferent or distant. Bowlby believed that early relationships, particularly with our primary caregivers, shape how we connect with others throughout our lives. Essentially, the way you attached to your caregivers as a child has a powerful influence on how you attach to people as an adult.

Think of attachment as the foundation for all future relationships. If you were raised in an environment where you felt safe, loved, and secure, you're more likely to develop healthy, balanced relationships later in life. On the flip side, if your caregivers were inconsistent, unavailable, or overly critical, you might find yourself struggling with fears of abandonment, or you may avoid emotional closeness altogether.

In other words, how you learned to connect with the people who mattered most as a child sets the stage for your relationship patterns as an adult. But here's the good news: just because you may have developed certain attachment habits doesn't mean you're stuck with them forever. Understanding your attachment style is the first step toward creating more secure, healthy connections.

What Bowlby discovered, and what countless studies since have confirmed, is that attachment is not just about childhood—it's something we carry with us into our adult relationships. And that's where things can get tricky, especially if your early experiences left you feeling anxious or uncertain in relationships. The good news is that while attachment patterns can be deeply ingrained, they are also adaptable. You can change, and that's exactly what we'll explore throughout this book.

By taking a close look at where your attachment style came from and how it developed, you'll gain clarity on why you feel and behave the way you do in relationships today. Understanding the origins of your attachment style helps you identify what's working, what's not, and how to start building the secure, loving connections you deserve.

This is where your journey of self-discovery begins. So, let's continue by exploring the different attachment styles and how they play out in our adult lives.

Different Attachment Styles

Now that we've touched on where attachment comes from, let's dive into the different types of attachment styles and what they mean for your relationships. By recognizing your own style, you'll begin to see patterns in how you connect with others—and that's key to making meaningful changes.

Anxious Attachment

If you've picked up this book, there's a good chance you may identify with the anxious attachment style. People with this style often feel a constant fear that their partner will leave or stop loving them. You might notice yourself overthinking every little thing in a relationship—worrying about whether your partner really cares, getting anxious when they don't respond right away, or feeling uneasy when they need space.

Anxious attachment often stems from inconsistent caregiving in childhood—maybe your parents were loving at times but unavailable or distant at others. As a result, you may have grown up feeling unsure whether love and support would be there when you needed it. This inconsistency creates a deep need for reassurance in adult relationships, making you more prone to feelings of insecurity and anxiety.

It's important to remember: anxious attachment doesn't make you "needy" or "too much." It's simply a pattern you learned early on, and with the right tools, you can break free from it.

Avoidant Attachment

On the other end of the spectrum is avoidant attachment. If you have this style, you probably value independence and emotional distance. You might find yourself feeling uncomfortable with too much closeness or intimacy, or you may be quick to pull away when someone gets too close.

Avoidant attachment typically develops when caregivers were emotionally unavailable or discouraged emotional expression. This can lead to a deep-seated belief that relying on others is unsafe or that intimacy will inevitably lead to disappointment. As a result, avoidantly attached individuals tend to keep relationships at arm's length.

If this sounds familiar, don't worry. You're not alone, and it's not something you can't change. Recognizing these tendencies is the first step toward building deeper, more secure connections.

Secure Attachment

Finally, there's secure attachment. People with this attachment style are generally comfortable with both closeness and independence. They trust their partner, can communicate openly, and feel confident in their relationships. If you have a secure attachment style, you likely grew up in an environment where your emotional needs were met consistently, giving you a sense of security and stability.

That said, many of us don't start out with a secure attachment style, and that's okay. The goal isn't to feel bad about where you are but to recognize that you can move toward secure attachment with time, patience, and the right tools. Even if you currently identify with anxious or avoidant attachment, you can learn to develop the skills and mindset of a securely attached person.

In the chapters to come, we'll go deeper into how each of these attachment styles impacts your day-to-day life and relationships.

And more importantly, we'll guide you through the steps to shift from anxious or avoidant patterns to a more secure, confident approach to love and connection.

Understanding your attachment style is just the beginning. Once you know where you stand, you'll be empowered to start making real, lasting changes in your relationships.

How Early Relationships Shape Adult Attachment Styles

Now that you have a sense of the different attachment styles, it's time to explore how those patterns were likely shaped by your earliest relationships. This can be an emotional topic for many of us because it means looking back at how we were raised, but remember, this is about understanding, not blaming. Our childhoods provide clues, not answers set in stone, about why we behave the way we do in our adult relationships.

The Blueprint from Childhood

The way we attach to people as adults is strongly influenced by the bonds we formed with our caregivers when we were children. These early relationships act as a blueprint for how we expect love and connection to work later in life. Whether you had parents who were attentive or distant, consistent or unpredictable, warm or emotionally unavailable—those experiences left an imprint.

For example, if your caregivers responded to your needs with love and consistency, you likely felt secure, knowing that someone would be there when you needed comfort. This can lead to a secure attachment style in adulthood. But if your caregivers were inconsistent—sometimes nurturing, other times absent—you might've learned to worry about when or if your needs would be met. This uncertainty often fosters anxious attachment.

On the other hand, if emotional support was unavailable or discouraged, you may have learned to rely solely on yourself, resulting in avoidant attachment. As a child, it might have felt safer to shut down emotionally rather than risk being hurt by unmet needs.

Recreating What Feels Familiar

Here's the tricky part: as adults, we often seek out or recreate the kind of relationships that feel familiar to us, even if they weren't healthy. It's not uncommon for people with anxious attachment to find themselves drawn to partners who are emotionally distant or inconsistent, mimicking the uncertainty they experienced growing up. Similarly, those with avoidant attachment may shy away from emotional closeness, just as they did in childhood.

This isn't something we do consciously—it's a pattern deeply rooted in how we've learned to connect with others. The good news is that these patterns aren't permanent. While early relationships set the stage, we can rewrite the script.

Rewriting Your Attachment Story

As we move forward in this book, we'll help you identify how your childhood relationships shaped your attachment style and, more importantly, how to break free from the patterns that no longer serve you. Recognizing the impact of your past is just the beginning. With the tools you'll learn in the coming chapters, you can start to build healthier, more secure relationships that reflect the person you are now, not the experiences you had then.

Remember, your attachment style doesn't define you. It's simply a starting point—a place to begin understanding why you respond to relationships the way you do. From here, you'll be equipped to change the way you love and connect, creating a future that feels safer, more stable, and full of trust.

Let's keep moving forward, together. You've already taken the first step.

CHAPTER 2: IDENTIFYING YOUR ATTACHMENT STYLE

Self-assessment quiz

Before we dive deeper into the work of healing, it's crucial to start with self-awareness. The best way to begin is by identifying your own attachment style. This isn't about labeling yourself, but rather understanding the patterns that may be influencing your relationships. Once you know what your attachment style is, you can take steps toward change.

This quick self-assessment will help you determine which attachment style—anxious, avoidant, or secure—feels most familiar to you. As you go through the questions, think about your behaviors, thoughts, and emotions when it comes to your closest relationships, particularly romantic ones. Be honest with yourself—there are no right or wrong answers here, just insight.

Quiz: What's Your Attachment Style?

Answer the following questions with a simple **"Yes"** or **"No."**

1. *I often worry that my partner doesn't love me or might leave me.* **Yes** ___ **No** ___

- Do you find yourself frequently feeling anxious about whether your partner truly cares for you or might abandon the relationship? This could be a sign of anxious attachment.

2. *I need a lot of reassurance from my partner that they care about me.* **Yes** ___ **No** ___

- Do you seek constant affirmation to feel secure in your relationship? If so, you might lean toward anxious attachment.

3. *I tend to avoid emotional intimacy, even when I care deeply about someone.* **Yes** ___ **No** ___

- Do you often keep your emotional distance to protect yourself from being hurt? This could suggest avoidant attachment.

4. *I have trouble depending on others, even when I need support.* **Yes** ___ **No** ___

- If you prefer to rely on yourself and feel uncomfortable depending on your partner for emotional support, you may have an avoidant attachment style.

5. *When my partner pulls away, I tend to get very anxious or upset.* **Yes __ No __**

- Do you feel a sense of panic or intense emotional reaction when your partner is distant or unresponsive? This is a common sign of anxious attachment.

6. *I feel uncomfortable when my partner wants to get too close too quickly.* **Yes __ No __**

- Do you push people away when the relationship feels too emotionally intense or intimate? This is often linked to avoidant attachment.

7. *I'm comfortable with intimacy and don't often worry about my relationships.* **Yes __ No __**

- If you can form close bonds without worrying about being abandoned or overwhelmed, you likely have a secure attachment style.

8. *I tend to think my partner should just "know" what I need without me having to ask.* **Yes __ No __**

- If you expect your partner to instinctively understand your emotional needs and get upset when they don't, it could be a sign of anxious attachment.

9. *When things go wrong, I often feel like it's my fault, even if my partner doesn't say so.* **Yes __ No __**

- Do you blame yourself when there's conflict in the relationship, assuming you must have done something wrong? This behavior often aligns with anxious attachment.

10. *I'm generally happy in my relationships and don't often worry about being abandoned.* **Yes __ No __**

- If this describes you, it's likely that you have a secure attachment style, allowing you to enjoy stable, trusting relationships.

Your Results

Now, let's look at your answers.

- *Mostly "Yes" to Questions 1, 2, 5, 8, or 9?* You may lean toward anxious attachment. This means you're likely to seek constant reassurance in relationships, feel worried about abandonment, and may experience a lot of emotional highs and lows.

- *Mostly "Yes" to Questions 3, 4, 6?* You might have an avoidant attachment. This could suggest you tend to keep your emotional distance, preferring independence over intimacy, even when in a close relationship.

- *Mostly "Yes" to Questions 7 and 10?* You probably have a secure attachment. You're comfortable with intimacy, don't fear abandonment, and are able to maintain healthy, balanced relationships.

Understanding Your Style

Your attachment style is like a map for how you navigate relationships. If you leaned toward anxious or avoidant attachment, don't worry—this isn't a fixed part of your personality. It's just the starting point for understanding your relationship habits. With the right tools, you can begin moving toward a more secure and balanced attachment style.

In the following chapters, we'll dive deeper into what your specific attachment style means for your relationships and, most importantly, how you can begin shifting it to create the loving, secure connection you deserve.

You're not alone in this journey, and just by reading this, you're already taking the first step toward understanding yourself more deeply. Keep going—you've got this!

Red Flags in Relationships

If you've ever found yourself feeling overly anxious, insecure, or even a bit obsessed in relationships, you might be dealing with some signs of anxious attachment. These feelings can sneak into your everyday interactions, creating emotional turmoil and making relationships more difficult than they need to be. But don't worry—acknowledging these behaviors is the first step toward change. Let's break down some of the common red flags that might show up if you're experiencing anxious attachment.

1. Constantly Needing Reassurance

Do you often feel the need to ask your partner, "Do you really love me?" or "Are we okay?" repeatedly? It's completely natural to want to feel loved, but with anxious attachment, the need for validation can become excessive. You might find yourself constantly seeking reassurance, even when there's no real sign that something's wrong. It can be exhausting for both you and your partner, leaving you feeling unsettled and unsure, no matter how much love you receive.

2. Fear of Abandonment

Does the idea of your partner leaving—whether it's breaking up or even just spending time apart—fill you with dread? This fear of abandonment is a hallmark of anxious attachment. You might worry that if they don't text you back immediately, or if they're busy with other commitments, they're going to disappear from your life altogether. This intense anxiety can lead to overthinking, worst-case scenarios, and even pushing your partner away to keep them close.

3. Overanalyzing Every Little Thing

Do you find yourself reading into every single thing your partner does or says? Maybe they seem quiet one day, and you immediately think they're upset with you, or you notice a change in their tone and assume they're losing interest. This kind of overanalysis is common in anxious attachment, where even small, insignificant details can spiral into major concerns in your mind. It creates unnecessary stress and tension in your relationship, often causing more problems than there really are.

4. Emotional Roller Coaster

Do your emotions swing wildly depending on how your partner is behaving? One minute, you're on top of the world because they sent you a sweet text. The next, you're spiraling into panic because they haven't responded for a few hours. These emotional highs and lows can leave you feeling unstable and uncertain in the relationship. Anxious attachment often creates a pattern where your sense of security is tied to your partner's actions, making it hard to feel grounded.

5. Difficulty Trusting Your Partner

Do you struggle to trust that your partner has your best interests at heart? Even when they've done nothing wrong, you might find yourself questioning their loyalty, intentions, or commitment. This lack of trust doesn't come from your partner's behavior—it stems from your own anxiety and fear of being hurt. Unfortunately, it can lead to behaviors like jealousy, controlling tendencies, or snooping, all of which can strain your relationship further.

6. Losing Yourself in the Relationship

Have you ever noticed that you start to revolve your whole world around your partner? With anxious attachment, there's a tendency to prioritize the relationship so much that you start to lose sight of your own needs, hobbies, and identity. You might feel like you can't be happy unless your partner is around or constantly thinking about how to please them. This dependency can lead to burnout and resentment, making it hard to maintain a balanced, healthy connection.

7. Fear of Conflict

Do you avoid bringing up issues because you're afraid it will upset your partner or push them away? Many people with anxious attachment are terrified of conflict, often suppressing their own needs or emotions to keep the peace. While it might seem like avoiding conflict is a good way to maintain harmony, it usually leads to resentment and unspoken frustration, which can build up over time and damage the relationship.

These red flags of anxious attachment don't mean there's something wrong with you or your relationship—they're just signals that there's room for growth and healing. It's important to recognize these patterns so you can work on shifting them. Remember, you're not stuck with these behaviors forever. The tools and insights in this book will guide you toward healthier, more secure attachment patterns, where you feel confident, loved, and secure in your relationships without the anxiety weighing you down. You're already on the right path by being here, and the steps ahead will help you get even closer to the kind of relationships you deserve.

Attachment Behaviors

Attachment behaviors can sometimes feel like a mystery—why do we react the way we do, or why does our partner behave in a certain way during emotional moments? Recognizing these patterns, both in yourself and in your partner, is a key part of developing healthier, more secure relationships. Once you understand these behaviors, you'll be better equipped to navigate emotional triggers and respond with more awareness and compassion.

1. Noticing Patterns in Your Reactions

Take a moment to think about how you typically respond when your partner seems distant or when conflict arises. Do you feel anxious, like you need to fix the situation immediately, or do you withdraw to avoid further confrontation? If you're anxiously attached, you might notice yourself trying to get closer to your partner whenever there's tension. This could look like sending several texts in a row, seeking reassurance, or feeling panicked when they don't respond quickly. These reactions can tell you a lot about your own attachment style.

On the other hand, avoidant attachment may show up as distancing behaviors—feeling overwhelmed by your partner's emotional needs or pulling back when things get too intense. If this sounds like your partner, recognizing these behaviors can help you understand why they might need more space at certain times. It's not that they don't care, but they may feel flooded by too much emotional closeness.

2. Emotional Triggers

What situations tend to bring out the most emotion in you or your partner? Are there specific moments that make you feel particularly vulnerable or insecure? For those with anxious attachment, emotional triggers often revolve around fears of rejection or abandonment. This might manifest as feeling upset when plans change unexpectedly, or when you don't hear from your partner for a while, leading to a fear that they're losing interest.

Your partner may also have their own emotional triggers based on their attachment style. If they're more avoidant, they might get triggered by too much closeness or feel anxious when they perceive pressure for emotional intimacy. Understanding these triggers can help you both approach emotional moments with greater empathy and awareness, rather than reacting automatically.

3. Communication Style

Pay attention to how you and your partner communicate during tough times. Do you find yourself expressing your emotions openly, hoping for reassurance? Or do you tend to hold back, worrying that your feelings might be too much for your partner to handle?

Anxiously attached individuals often crave open, frequent communication, while avoidant individuals may prefer to keep things more low-key, avoiding deep conversations unless absolutely necessary.

If you feel like you're constantly initiating conversations about the relationship or needing to address your concerns, this could be a sign of anxious attachment. On the flip side, if your partner seems to avoid these conversations or gets uncomfortable when emotions run high, they may have more avoidant tendencies. Neither of these styles is "wrong," but they can create friction if both partners aren't aware of these differences.

4. Managing Conflict

How do you and your partner handle conflict? Do you feel like you need to resolve it immediately to regain a sense of security, or do you (or your partner) tend to withdraw, needing time alone to process? If you're anxiously attached, unresolved conflict can feel deeply unsettling, pushing you to seek resolution quickly, sometimes at the expense of your emotional well-being. In contrast, an avoidantly attached partner might need more time to cool off, and they might distance themselves until they feel ready to re-engage.

Recognizing these differences in how you and your partner manage conflict is crucial. If you're anxious, try to give your partner the space they need without feeling like the relationship is at risk. If your partner is anxious, reassure them that time apart isn't a sign of detachment, but rather a way to reset and come back to the issue with a clearer mind.

5. Physical and Emotional Closeness

Another key to recognizing attachment behaviors lies in how you both approach physical and emotional closeness. For anxious attachment, there's often a strong need for closeness, affection, and frequent contact to feel secure. You might feel unsettled or lonely when your partner isn't around, or you may crave more touch and words of affirmation to feel connected.

If your partner leans more avoidant, they might enjoy closeness too, but in measured doses. You might notice that after a day of being very affectionate, they suddenly pull back or need more personal space. Recognizing these patterns without taking them personally can help you both find a rhythm that feels good and respectful to both of you.

Understanding your attachment style—and your partner's—can open up new levels of empathy and communication. You'll start to see why certain situations trigger anxiety or distance, and more importantly, how to work together to create balance. Remember, these behaviors don't define your relationship; they're just habits that can be shifted with the right tools and mindset. This book will guide you through that process, step by step, so you and your partner can find deeper connection and security.

CHAPTER 3: ATTACHMENT STYLES IN ACTION

Real-Life Examples

When we talk about attachment styles, it can sometimes feel abstract, like it's just something in a psychology book. But these patterns show up in real, everyday relationships. You might even recognize them in your own life. Let's walk through what anxious, avoidant, and secure attachment styles can look like in action.

Anxious Attachment: Constantly Seeking Reassurance

Meet Sarah and Alex. Sarah loves Alex deeply, but she often feels a sense of insecurity in their relationship. She tends to send multiple texts when Alex doesn't reply right away, asking if everything is okay, even when there's no reason to worry. Sometimes, Sarah feels jealous when Alex spends time with friends or doesn't invite her to every social event. She craves closeness and feels unsettled when Alex isn't available to reassure her.

For Sarah, even small changes in Alex's behavior can trigger a lot of anxiety. When Alex has a busy day at work and doesn't respond to her messages, Sarah's mind spirals into worry—Is Alex losing interest? Did I do something wrong? This constant need for reassurance takes a toll on Sarah's self-esteem, and over time, it starts to affect their relationship.

This is an example of anxious attachment in action. Sarah's fear of being abandoned makes her hyper-vigilant to any perceived distance from Alex, which can lead to a cycle of needing more reassurance and feeling more anxious when she doesn't get it.

Avoidant Attachment: Guarding Emotional Distance

Now, let's look at James and Emily. James is a caring partner, but he values his independence above all. He's not one to talk about his feelings, and when Emily tries to get him to open up, James often changes the subject or withdraws. He loves spending time with her, but after a few days of deep connection, he feels the need to retreat, either by focusing on work or spending time alone.

When conflicts arise, James tends to shut down emotionally. Instead of talking things through with Emily, he might take hours (or even days) to process his feelings in private. Emily often feels like she's walking on eggshells, unsure of when James might pull away again.

This is a common pattern for avoidant attachment. James cares about Emily, but his fear of being overwhelmed by emotional closeness makes him instinctively create distance when things start to feel too intimate. Over time, this can make it hard for to feel truly connected.

Secure Attachment: Balanced and Trusting

Finally, let's look at a secure couple, Jenna and Mike. Jenna and Mike have their ups and downs like any other couple, but they're able to communicate openly when issues arise. If Mike is feeling stressed at work, he tells Jenna how he's feeling instead of shutting her out. Jenna, in turn, supports him without feeling like she has to solve all his problems. They trust each other, and when disagreements happen, they both feel secure enough to talk things through without fearing the relationship is in danger.

Jenna doesn't worry if Mike takes a little longer to reply to her messages, and Mike feels comfortable expressing his needs for alone time without worrying that Jenna will feel abandoned. There's a sense of mutual respect and emotional balance in their relationship.

This is what secure attachment looks like. Both partners are able to give and receive emotional support in a healthy, trusting way. They can be close without feeling suffocated and independent without fearing abandonment.

These real-life examples show how different attachment styles can play out in relationships. Whether you see yourself in Sarah's anxious tendencies, James's avoidant behavior, or Jenna and Mike's secure connection, understanding these dynamics is the first step toward healthier, more fulfilling relationships.

This book will help you identify where you are on this spectrum and guide you toward creating a more secure and balanced attachment style, so you can enjoy deeper, more trusting connections.

The Emotional Rollercoaster

If you've experienced anxious attachment, you know that it often feels like being on an emotional rollercoaster. One moment, you're filled with love, excitement, and a deep connection with your partner. But the next, a small shift—like a delayed text or a change in tone—can send your emotions spiraling into anxiety and insecurity. It's exhausting, isn't it? This constant fluctuation between highs and lows can take a toll not only on your mental health but also on your relationship.

The Highs: Closeness and Connection

When things are going well, anxious attachment can make you feel incredibly close to your partner. You might find yourself basking in moments of affection, feeling like you're on top of the world when your partner is giving you the attention and validation you crave. You feel secure, loved, and important. It's in these moments that your relationship feels perfect.

But for many of us with anxious attachment, these highs come with an unspoken fear: What if this doesn't last? You might start to wonder when the next drop in the emotional ride will come. Even in the best moments, there's often a nagging sense of uncertainty lurking in the background.

The Lows: Doubt, Anxiety, and Fear of Rejection
And then there are the lows—those moments when your partner seems distant, distracted, or just not as engaged as you hoped. This is when the emotional rollercoaster takes a nosedive. You might start to overthink: Why are they pulling away? Did I say something wrong? Are they losing interest?

The anxiety can snowball quickly, causing you to cling more tightly to your partner or become overly focused on getting reassurance. You might ask for constant affirmations of love, feel jealous of their time with others, or even push them away out of fear that they'll eventually leave you. All of this happens because your brain is wired to protect you from rejection, but it often leads to more emotional turmoil.

Feeling Out of Control

One of the hardest parts of anxious attachment is feeling like your emotions are constantly at the mercy of your partner's behavior. When they're close and attentive, you're happy and secure. But when they're distant or preoccupied, it feels like your entire emotional foundation crumbles. It's as if you're handing over control of your happiness and self-worth to someone else—and that can feel terrifying.

This rollercoaster creates a cycle of dependency, where your mood and sense of security are tied to your partner's actions. You may find yourself becoming overly sensitive to their moods, constantly checking in to make sure everything's okay, or even avoiding conflict to prevent them from pulling away.

Breaking Free from the Ride

The good news? You don't have to stay on this emotional rollercoaster forever. By understanding how anxious attachment affects your relationships, you can start to untangle these intense emotional reactions. The key is recognizing the patterns and learning new ways to soothe your anxiety that don't rely on constant reassurance from your partner.

Throughout this book, we'll guide you through strategies to calm your anxious mind, build emotional resilience, and regain control over your feelings. It's about stepping off the rollercoaster and finding stability, so you can enjoy your relationships without the constant emotional swings.

You deserve to feel secure and confident in your relationships, and together, I'll help you get there.

Observe Attachment Styles

Observing your own attachment style can feel a bit like putting a mirror up to your relationships and seeing things more clearly, sometimes for the first time. This might feel vulnerable at first, but it's also a powerful way to understand how you connect with others and respond in relationships. The more you learn to spot these patterns, the more control you'll have over how you relate to others, which is an empowering place to be.

Start Noticing Patterns in Your Thoughts and Reactions

When it comes to attachment, our internal dialogue often holds the first clues. For instance, do you find yourself feeling panicked if your partner doesn't respond to a text as quickly as you'd like? Or, if they seem distracted, do you jump to worst-case scenarios? These thought patterns are typical signs of anxious attachment, where we can experience heightened fears of abandonment and rejection.

Try this exercise: Next time you feel anxious in your relationship, pause and ask yourself what exactly triggered that feeling. Was it something your partner did or didn't do? Identifying these triggers helps you get to the root of your attachment behaviors.

Observe Your Reactions in Moments of Distance or Closeness
Attachment styles can show up most clearly in moments when closeness fluctuates—whether it's physical, emotional, or even digital (like a partner not texting back right away). For example, if you lean towards anxious attachment, you might feel a strong urge to reach out and reconnect whenever there's a bit of distance. On the flip side, someone with an avoidant style might pull back when things get too close or intense.

By simply noticing how you feel and act in these moments of closeness and distance, you'll start to see your unique attachment style in action. Observe how you respond without judgment—are you feeling drawn to reach out for reassurance, or are you tempted to create some space to feel safer? Just noticing is a big step.

Identify Attachment-Based Triggers in Conflict

Conflict has a way of bringing out our attachment needs. When you and your partner disagree, what's your immediate reaction? If you find yourself worried that the argument might damage your relationship, this can be a sign of anxious attachment. On the other hand, feeling the need to withdraw and avoid the conversation altogether could indicate avoidant tendencies.

Try paying attention to the emotions and thoughts that come up during these moments. Are you worried about being left or unloved? Or are you focused on maintaining your independence and freedom? Recognizing these patterns in conflict can give you deep insights into your attachment style.

Take Note of Your Partner's Attachment Style Too

Your partner's attachment behaviors will also impact your relationship dynamic. Start paying attention to how they react in moments of closeness, distance, or conflict. Do they seem comfortable with emotional closeness, or do they avoid it? Are they quick to reassure you, or do they tend to pull away when things get intense? Recognizing your partner's attachment style can help you better understand how the two of you interact and may help you empathize with their perspective.

Practicing Self-Compassion as You Observe

Observing your attachment style isn't about finding fault in yourself; it's about understanding where certain patterns come from so you can respond more thoughtfully in relationships. Remind yourself that these behaviors developed to cope, to protect yourself, or to try to create connection. The goal here is gentle awareness. As you become more in tune with these behaviors, you'll be better equipped to make choices that lead to healthier, more fulfilling relationships.

PART 2: OVERCOMING FEAR OF REJECTION AND ABANDONMENT

CHAPTER 4: BREAKING FREE FROM FEAR OF ABANDONMENT

Fear of abandonment is a deep-seated feeling, often rooted in experiences from our past. If you've ever felt an overwhelming worry that someone you care about might leave, or if you find yourself second-guessing their commitment to you, you're certainly not alone. This chapter dives into the *"why"* behind that fear and gives you tools to start loosening its grip on your relationships.

Understanding the Roots of Abandonment Fear

Abandonment fear often begins in early relationships with caregivers. When we're young, we rely entirely on those closest to us for love, support, and safety. If these needs aren't consistently met, we may begin to fear that love is conditional or that people will leave, leaving us unprepared to handle being alone. Even if abandonment didn't happen, inconsistency—such as parents or caregivers being emotionally unavailable—can create an underlying worry that love and security are temporary.

As adults, these fears often resurface in romantic relationships and friendships, where the stakes feel high, and rejection seems painful. Even when our rational minds tell us a partner cares about us, that old, familiar fear can surface unexpectedly. These feelings can be incredibly frustrating, especially because they don't always match what's happening in our present-day relationships.

The Fear Cycle

One of the hardest parts of abandonment fear is that it tends to reinforce itself. Here's how it works: we worry about being abandoned, which leads us to seek constant reassurance or act in ways that, ironically, can push people away. Then, if our partner seems even slightly distant or if a friend doesn't respond as warmly as we hope, we may interpret it as a sign they're pulling away. The fear kicks in stronger, and we seek more reassurance or control in the relationship, continuing the cycle.

Over time, this fear-driven cycle can create a lot of stress in relationships. It's exhausting to live on edge, and it's equally tough for those around us to constantly offer reassurance. The good news is that recognizing the cycle is the first step to breaking it.

The Psychology Behind Fear of Abandonment

On a psychological level, fear of abandonment can stem from our brain's survival instinct. When our early experiences left us feeling insecure, our minds learned to associate closeness with safety—and separation or distance with danger. So, when a partner or loved one seems distant, it's as though our brains sound an alarm, alerting us to the "danger" of losing love and support. This is why even minor situations, like a delayed text or a quiet response, can feel surprisingly intense.

Our thoughts in these moments may become hyper-focused on what's wrong, jumping to conclusions that someone is upset, disappointed, or even thinking of leaving. Without realizing it, we may catastrophize, mentally preparing ourselves for the worst. These thoughts are part of what psychologists call "attachment insecurity," and they're common in people with anxious attachment styles. Recognizing that these thoughts are a natural (but sometimes exaggerated) response is essential.

The Path Forward

Breaking free from abandonment fear means learning to reshape these deeply ingrained responses. In this chapter, we'll work through strategies to:

- **Challenge abandonment-focused thoughts:** Shifting from *"I know they're going to leave"* to *"I'm feeling anxious because I care about this relationship, but that doesn't mean anything is wrong."*

- **Develop self-soothing techniques:** Building confidence in handling tough emotions, so you don't always rely on external reassurance.

- **Strengthen your sense of self:** By cultivating your self-worth, you'll begin to see that even if a relationship changes, you are capable, resilient, and worthy.

As you work through this, remember: overcoming abandonment fears is a journey, not an overnight fix. This process is about replacing old, unhelpful responses with new, empowering ones. Each time you take a step towards understanding and challenging these fears, you're reclaiming your peace of mind and giving yourself the chance to build healthier, more fulfilling connections.

How Fear Drives Emotions

When fear of abandonment is present, it doesn't just sit quietly in the background—it stirs up some of the toughest feelings we experience in relationships: jealousy, insecurity, and anxiety. If you're familiar with these emotions, you know they can seem to pop up out of nowhere, even when things are going well. Let's unpack how fear fuels these feelings and what we can start doing about it.

The Link Between Fear and Jealousy

Jealousy often comes from a fear of losing something or someone important to us. When we worry about abandonment, we might feel especially threatened by others who seem to get attention from the people we care about. It can be subtle at first—a friend praising someone else, a partner chatting with a new coworker—but our brains can quickly turn these small things into big worries. Thoughts like *"What if they like them more than me?"* or *"Am I not enough?"* creep in, leading to a sense of jealousy that's rooted more in fear than reality.

These moments can feel frustrating because deep down, we might realize our jealousy is more about our own fears than the actions of our partner or friend. But knowing this doesn't always make it easier to manage! By exploring the fear behind jealousy, we can start seeing it for what it is: a signal of our attachment anxiety rather than proof that someone else is a threat.

How Fear Fuels Insecurity

Fear of abandonment can make us question our worth and wonder if we're enough. This insecurity often plays out in self-doubt, constantly second-guessing how lovable or valuable we are. In relationships, insecurity might sound like a little voice saying, *"What if they find someone better?"* or *"Why would they stay with me?"* Over time, this can lead to us feeling overly sensitive to any sign of disinterest or distance, no matter how small.

Because our self-worth is fragile in moments of insecurity, we end up looking outside ourselves for validation. This is when we might ask for reassurance more often than usual, seek approval, or worry excessively about what our partner or friend thinks. But the truth is, no amount of external validation can completely erase these insecurities. We need to work from the inside out, building a stronger foundation that isn't shaken by small shifts in attention or affection.

The Anxiety Spiral: A Fear of Loss Loop

Fear, jealousy, and insecurity can create a loop of anxiety that's hard to break out of. Anxiety in relationships is often fueled by a mix of worry about the future, fear of potential rejection, and doubts about our self-worth. When we're in this anxious state, it can be tempting to analyze every interaction, seeking clues that someone might be pulling away or preparing to leave. We might even interpret neutral events as signs that something is wrong.

This anxiety doesn't just live in our thoughts; it often shows up in our bodies, too. Racing heartbeats, nervous energy, or even feeling "on edge" are common physical responses to the worry of being abandoned. Anxiety in relationships can make us feel like we're in constant fight-or-flight mode, as if we need to be ready to defend against loss at any moment.

Breaking Free from Fear-Driven Responses

Recognizing how fear drives these feelings is a powerful first step in breaking their hold on us. Once we see the pattern—fear leading to jealousy, insecurity, and anxiety—we can begin to choose new ways of responding. Here's what we'll work on throughout this book to manage and reduce these emotions:

- **Building internal validation:** So that we rely less on others to feel secure in who we are.
- **Practicing grounding techniques:** These can help calm our minds and bodies when we feel that anxiety spike.
- **Reframing jealousy as a signal:** We'll explore how to see jealousy as a signal to check in with ourselves rather than a cue to control or fix something in the relationship.

These steps don't erase the fear instantly, but they help us create a new relationship with it—one where we recognize the emotions without letting them control us. As we practice, we'll find that our relationships start feeling more secure and that we're able to approach them from a place of confidence and calm.

Recognizing When Fear Is Influencing Your Behavior

Fear is sneaky; it often shapes our actions in ways that feel so natural we don't even notice. When fear of abandonment is in the driver's seat, it can lead us to behave in ways we wouldn't otherwise choose. But learning to spot fear's influence is the key to breaking out of this cycle. This awareness gives us a chance to respond differently, with more confidence and calm. Here, we'll look at how fear might be showing up in your actions—and what to do about it.

The Subtle Signs of Fear-Based Actions

Fear can show up in ways that seem completely rational at the moment. Maybe you find yourself checking your partner's social media a bit too often or constantly seeking reassurance that they still care. You might feel the need to text them frequently just to "stay connected" or worry when they don't respond right away. These behaviors often come from a place of fear—fear that, left unchecked, might start running the show.

The tricky part is that these actions don't feel like fear; they often feel like attempts at "staying connected" or "keeping things stable." But if you pause to check in with yourself, you might notice a knot of anxiety beneath these actions, a feeling that you'll lose something important if you're not vigilant.

Questions to Help Spot Fear's Influence

To get a handle on when fear is guiding your actions, ask yourself a few reflective questions:

- **Why am I doing this?** If the answer is, "Because I'm afraid they'll leave" or "Because I need to know they still care," that's a strong signal fear is at play.
- **Would I act this way if I felt totally secure?** Imagining yourself in a fully secure state can reveal behaviors that don't actually serve you.
- **Am I trying to control or fix something?** Fear often pushes us to control or fix situations that feel uncertain. Recognizing this pattern helps you decide when to take a step back.

Asking yourself these questions in the moment can be challenging but worth it. Noticing these subtle cues opens the door to responding differently—taking a deep breath, stepping back, or simply sitting with the feeling without acting on it.

Building New Responses to Fear

Once you recognize when fear is showing up, you can start replacing fear-driven behaviors with responses that bring you closer to a secure, healthy connection. Here are some gentle steps you can try:

- **Pause before you act:** When you notice fear rising, take a moment to breathe deeply and ground yourself. This pause often helps reduce the urge to act out of anxiety.

- **Challenge the fear:** Remind yourself of your partner's actual actions and the trust you're building together, rather than letting old fears guide your reaction.

- **Shift your focus:** Sometimes, stepping back and focusing on something else—like a hobby or a friend—can help break the cycle of anxious thoughts and let the fear subside naturally.

Learning to recognize fear's influence takes time, but with practice, you'll start spotting it more easily. And each time you choose to pause, challenge, or shift, you're taking a big step toward breaking free from fear's grip. As you work through these moments, you're building trust in yourself, showing that you're capable of handling whatever comes up—and that's a huge step toward the resilience and security you're seeking.

CHAPTER 5: MANAGING ANXIETY IN RELATIONSHIPS

Tools for Reducing Anxiety

Anxiety in relationships can feel overwhelming, like a storm that won't let up. But here's the thing: there are tools that can help you calm that storm, ways to break the cycle of anxious thoughts so you can feel more at ease with yourself and your partner. Cognitive-behavioral techniques (CBT) are incredibly effective for this. They offer practical, step-by-step approaches to manage anxiety and bring a sense of control back into your life.

How Cognitive-Behavioral Techniques Work

CBT works by targeting the thoughts and beliefs that fuel anxiety. Often, anxiety arises not from what's happening around us, but from how we interpret those events. For example, a partner's delayed response might spark thoughts like, "They're losing interest" or "They're upset with me." CBT helps you examine these thoughts, question their truth, and replace them with ones that are more realistic and supportive.

Let's break down some simple CBT tools that you can start using right away. The goal isn't to deny or suppress your feelings but to understand and manage them in ways that serve your peace of mind and allow for healthier connections.

1. Identifying Automatic Thoughts

Automatic thoughts are those initial responses that pop up without us even noticing. They're fast, often intense, and can amplify anxiety. When you're feeling anxious, the first step is to notice these automatic thoughts as they come up. Maybe it's a worry that you're being ignored, or a feeling that you're not valued. Just by becoming aware of these thoughts, you're taking the first step in managing them.

- **Practice**: Next time anxiety surfaces, pause and identify the thought that came before it. Write it down if you can, as seeing it on paper can make it feel less overwhelming.

2. Challenging Anxious Thoughts

Once you've identified an anxious thought, the next step is to challenge it. Ask yourself if it's based on facts or assumptions. Anxiety often skews things, making us interpret situations more negatively than we would if we were calm.

- **Questions to ask yourself**: Is there concrete evidence for this thought? Have I felt this way before in similar situations? What would I say to a friend who was feeling this way?

By challenging the thought, you're giving yourself a chance to see things from a new perspective—one that's less driven by fear.

3. Replacing Negative Thoughts with Balanced Ones

Once you've challenged an anxious thought, try replacing it with something more balanced and supportive. For example, instead of thinking, "They don't care about me," you might try, "They could be busy, but that doesn't mean they don't care." Balanced thoughts like these offer a middle ground—they don't ignore the worry, but they also don't let it take over.

- **Practice**: Write down a few supportive thoughts you can return to when anxiety flares up. These "go-to" thoughts can help keep you grounded in moments when your mind wants to spiral.

4. Practicing Self-Compassion

When anxiety hits, it's easy to feel frustrated with yourself for even feeling anxious in the first place. But being hard on yourself only increases the stress. Instead, practice self-compassion. Remind yourself that managing anxiety is a journey, and that every step you take counts, no matter how small.

- **Try this**: Next time you notice anxiety, place a hand on your heart or take a deep breath and say something kind to yourself, like "I'm doing the best I can" or "It's okay to feel this way." Self-compassion is like giving yourself a warm blanket of understanding.

Learning to use CBT tools takes practice, but each time you apply them, you're building a stronger foundation for emotional resilience. With time, these tools can help you respond to anxiety in ways that support both your peace and the health of your relationships. Remember, the goal isn't to eliminate all worries—it's to bring them down to a level that doesn't overshadow the love and connection you want to experience.

Techniques to Halt Negative Spirals

We've all been there—one small worry creeps in, then another, and before you know it, you're in a full-on spiral of negative thoughts. Maybe it starts with a simple text that goes unanswered, and soon you're convinced the relationship is doomed. These spirals don't just drain your energy; they fuel your anxiety, making it hard to see things as they really are. Thought-stopping techniques are a way to interrupt this cycle before it gains momentum.

Thought-stopping is exactly what it sounds like—a way to put the brakes on anxious thoughts before they derail your peace. Let's explore how to use this technique to feel more grounded and focused.

1. Recognize the Onset of Negative Spirals

The first step is awareness. Notice the moment you start feeling anxious, and catch the thought that triggered it. Sometimes these thoughts come in subtly and build up, but you can train yourself to become aware earlier and earlier in the process.

- Quick tip: The next time you feel a negative thought building, try silently saying to yourself, "I'm spiraling." This helps you recognize that you're in a cycle and that you have the power to interrupt it.

2. Practice the "Stop" Technique

Once you catch a negative thought, firmly tell yourself, "Stop." Say it out loud if you're alone, or visualize a big red "Stop" sign if you're in public. This may sound simple, but this visual and verbal interruption can jolt your mind out of its anxious pattern and create a pause.

- Try this: Imagine your thoughts like a TV show you can pause or turn off. Every time you catch yourself spiraling, visualize hitting that "pause" button. It's a reminder that you're in control of what you choose to continue thinking.

3. Shift Focus with a Positive Distraction

After stopping the thought, the next step is to redirect your mind. Shifting focus can be anything from a quick walk, listening to a favorite song, or even doing a small task that requires your attention.

The idea isn't to avoid or deny the thought but to remind your mind that there's more out there than this single worry.

- Example: If you're out and about, find a small item to focus on—the color of a leaf, the sound of the breeze, or the smell of coffee. These small sensory shifts bring you back to the present and out of the spiral.

4. Replace the Thought with a Calming Phrase

Once you've put the brakes on the anxious thought, give your mind something calming to hold onto. It can be a reassuring phrase or a grounding affirmation that brings you peace and reminds you of your resilience.

- Try this: Repeat a phrase like "I am safe, and things will unfold as they should" or "I am capable of handling this moment." Repeating it a few times can create a calm center within the anxiety, helping you feel more in control.

5. Reflect on Your Success

Whenever you successfully stop a thought spiral, acknowledge it! These small victories add up over time, and recognizing them builds confidence. You're training your mind to step out of old patterns, one thought at a time.

- **Note to self:** Stopping a negative thought is a powerful action that shows you're growing. Keep a small journal or notes app entry where you jot down these moments to look back on as a reminder of your progress.

Thought-stopping isn't about dismissing your feelings or pretending the anxiety isn't there. It's about teaching yourself to handle the thoughts without letting them control you. It gives you the chance to pause, breathe, and choose how to respond instead of reacting out of fear. Every time you use thought-stopping, you're building a habit of self-compassion and reclaiming your peace, one thought at a time.

Emotion Regulation Strategies

When attachment anxiety starts bubbling up, it can feel like a tidal wave of emotions—fear, insecurity, even panic—all rushing in at once. This part is about finding ways to steady yourself, to manage those intense feelings without letting them take over. Emotion regulation isn't about ignoring your feelings but instead learning how to respond to them in ways that support and ground you. These strategies will help you create space between yourself and the emotional storm, allowing you to move through it with more calm and confidence.

1. Practice Deep Breathing to Ground Yourself

Anxiety often brings a sense of urgency or dread, which triggers shallow, quick breaths. Slowing down your breathing sends a signal to your nervous system that it's safe to relax, shifting your body out of "fight-or-flight" mode.

- **Try this**: Breathe in deeply for four counts, hold for four, and exhale for six. Repeat this a few times until you feel a shift in your energy. This simple technique is a quick way to steady yourself and return to the present moment.

2. Label Your Emotions Without Judging Them

Emotions can be overwhelming, especially when they arrive as an intense bundle of insecurity or worry. Taking a moment to label what you're feeling can help separate the emotion from your immediate reaction, giving you more control.

- **How to try it**: As feelings come up, name them without judging yourself. "I'm feeling insecure" or "I'm experiencing fear of abandonment." This allows you to witness your emotions rather than get caught up in them, a powerful way to remind yourself that feelings are temporary and manageable.

3. Reframe Negative Thoughts

Our thoughts often intensify our feelings of anxiety, especially when we jump to worst-case scenarios. Reframing is a way to gently challenge those thoughts, helping you see situations in a more balanced light.

- **Practice this**: When an anxious thought arises, ask yourself, "What's another way to look at this?" Instead of thinking, "They're pulling away from me," try reframing it to, "They may just be busy." This shift helps lessen the emotional intensity, keeping you calm and open-minded.

4. Engage in Physical Activity

Sometimes, our bodies hold onto anxiety, and moving can release some of that stored tension. Whether it's a short walk, stretching, or even a few minutes of dancing, physical activity can be a quick and effective reset.

- **Example**: When you notice anxiety creeping in, get up and move—even just for a couple of minutes. Physical activity not only helps clear your mind but also gives your body a chance to release nervous energy and recharge.

5. Use Self-Soothing Techniques

Self-soothing is about nurturing yourself in small ways to counterbalance anxious moments. This can be anything that comforts you, whether it's a warm drink, wrapping up in a cozy blanket, or listening to your favorite song.

- **Try this**: Create a list of your go-to self-soothing activities. When anxiety feels overwhelming, turn to one of them. This habit reminds you that you're capable of creating comfort for yourself, which builds resilience over time.

6. Cultivate Self-Compassion

When anxious thoughts and fears show up, they're often accompanied by self-criticism or shame. Instead, try treating yourself with the same kindness you'd offer a friend going through a tough time.

- **A small practice**: When self-criticism arises, respond with compassion. Say something like, "I'm doing the best I can, and it's okay to feel this way." Self-compassion helps you feel supported from within, reducing the intensity of anxious emotions.

These strategies are tools to have in your back pocket for those inevitable moments when anxiety rears its head. They help bring the focus back to you—your resilience, your ability to manage emotions, and your capacity to find calm. As you practice these techniques, you're building an emotional toolkit that supports healthier, more secure relationships with both yourself and others.

CHAPTER 6: HEALING THE INNER CHILD

Understanding the Role of Early Childhood Experiences in Attachment Issues

For many of us, our earliest experiences hold clues about the patterns we see in our adult relationships. Those foundational years—filled with our first experiences of love, safety, trust, and sometimes hurt—are like the groundwork that shapes how we connect with others as adults. This is where the concept of the *"inner child"* comes into play, representing those early parts of ourselves that may still be seeking the security, care, and acceptance we may not have fully received.

When we talk about "attachment," we're diving into a deep-seated drive within each of us, formed during our most formative years. This drive is influenced by how safe, supported, and seen we felt as children. If, in those early days, we experienced consistent love, support, and attention, it was easier to develop a sense of trust and security. On the flip side, if love and support felt unpredictable, conditional, or even absent, it can lead to attachment insecurities that stay with us into adulthood.

This isn't about blaming anyone or picking apart the past for the sake of it. Rather, it's about understanding where certain relationship fears, anxieties, or defenses come from so we can gently work with them. Recognizing that much of our adult attachment style is rooted in these early experiences can be incredibly freeing. It's a way of telling ourselves, *"This isn't my fault, but now that I see it, I can work with it."*

In this chapter, we'll look closely at the ways early childhood shapes our adult attachments, giving you a better understanding of where your fears, worries, or clingy tendencies may stem from. It's about learning to meet that inner child with kindness, offering the love and reassurance they might have missed. This is the foundation of healing, one that doesn't rewrite your past but allows you to choose a different future—one that's rooted in secure, trusting relationships.

Unresolved Emotional Wounds

When it comes to healing our attachment styles, one of the hardest but most important steps is addressing the emotional wounds we carry from our past. These wounds often stem from times when we didn't receive the support, understanding, or consistency we needed, which can linger as unresolved hurts that continue to influence how we view ourselves and our relationships. You're not alone in this— many people carry these invisible weights without even realizing it.

Addressing these wounds doesn't mean reliving every painful memory or assigning blame; rather, it's about offering compassion to the parts of yourself that still feel vulnerable or hurt. Think of it like tending to an old scar: it may have healed on the surface, but underneath, there's sensitivity that needs gentle care. Unresolved wounds can show up in our adult relationships as fears of abandonment, distrust, jealousy, or the urge to seek constant reassurance. Recognizing these responses as echoes of old hurts can help us break free from them.

To start this journey, here are some practical steps that can help:

- Acknowledge the Pain Without Judgment: Take a moment to accept these emotions without labeling them as "bad" or "wrong." When you feel triggered, try to step back and identify the feeling. This could be fear, shame, or sadness tied to the times you felt misunderstood or unsupported in the past. By identifying the emotion without criticism, you open the door to understanding it rather than avoiding it.

- Self-Compassion: Treat yourself with the same kindness you would show a close friend. Imagine what you would say to someone who shared the same experiences, and offer those words to yourself. Self-compassion is incredibly healing; it allows you to acknowledge pain while reassuring yourself that you're worthy of love and healing.

- Connect with Your Inner Child: This may sound a bit unusual, but visualizing and connecting with your "inner child" can be a powerful tool. Picture yourself at a young age—maybe a time when you felt most vulnerable. Imagine speaking to that younger self with the love, encouragement, and validation they may not have received. By offering reassurance to this inner child, you're giving yourself permission to grow beyond past limitations.

- Practice Mindful Forgiveness: Forgiveness, whether it's directed toward someone else or yourself, can help release the hold of old wounds. This doesn't mean condoning harmful behaviors but rather freeing yourself from the burden of carrying unresolved anger or resentment. It's about clearing the space for new, healthier attachments to grow.

Working through these emotional wounds takes time and patience. It's a process, not a one-time fix. Remember, each step you take toward understanding and soothing these hurts brings you closer to the kind of connection and trust you deserve in your relationships.

Healing is about reclaiming the parts of yourself that are ready to move forward, transforming old patterns into a future of healthier, more secure love.

Practical Exercises to Soothe and Heal Your Inner Child

Healing your inner child can be a deeply transformative part of your journey toward secure, healthy relationships. Sometimes, the past versions of ourselves—the ones that didn't feel safe, seen, or loved—need a bit of extra attention. By connecting with that younger part of yourself, you can bring healing and reassurance where it's been missing for a long time. Here are a few simple, yet powerful exercises designed to help you connect with and comfort your inner child.

1. Write a Letter to Your Younger Self

This exercise is like giving your inner child a direct line to your adult self, where you get to be the safe, understanding figure you needed back then. Grab a notebook or piece of paper and write a letter to yourself at an age when you felt particularly vulnerable. Think about the things that worried or hurt you, and use this space to reassure your younger self. Let them know they were never "too much" or "not enough," and that they deserved love and safety.

- **Example Prompts**:

- o *"Dear (your younger self's name or age), I know you felt scared and alone when... But I want you to know that you were doing the best you could. You didn't deserve to feel that way, and I'm here now to remind you that you're safe."*
  - o *"You are enough, just as you are. And I'm proud of you for making it through."*

2. Guided Visualization: Meeting Your Inner Child

In this exercise, you'll use visualization to meet your inner child in a safe, comforting setting. Find a quiet place where you won't be interrupted, close your eyes, and picture a warm, inviting space—maybe a childhood bedroom, a cozy forest, or a sunlit beach. Imagine meeting your younger self there. Visualize yourself sitting together, and let your inner child express anything they might feel. In this space, you can give them the love, protection, or comfort they may not have received before.

- **Dialogue Suggestions**:
  - o *"What do you need most right now? How can I help you feel safe?"*
  - o *"I'm here for you, and I'll always be here to listen."*

3. Mirror Work for Self-Reassurance

Standing in front of a mirror, look yourself in the eyes and speak words of comfort and affirmation directly to yourself. This can feel a little strange at first, but it's an incredibly powerful way to build self-compassion and self-worth. Imagine you're speaking to the younger you, providing encouragement and kindness. Affirmations like *"I am safe," "I am worthy of love,"* or *"I forgive myself"* can gently disrupt old patterns of self-criticism and help you build new beliefs about your worth.

4. Create a "Comfort Box" with Reminders of Safety

Build a physical reminder of the safety and support you're creating for yourself by putting together a "comfort box." Fill it with items that soothe you—like a soft blanket, a favorite book, photos of happy memories, or anything that brings you peace and comfort. When you're feeling anxious or triggered, take a moment to open this box and reconnect with these items as a reminder of the care you're providing for yourself now.

5. Daily Affirmations and Compassionate Reminders

Incorporate compassionate affirmations into your daily routine. These can be gentle reminders that help counteract feelings *of insecurity or fear. For example, start each day with a reminder: "I am healing and growing every day,"* or, *"I am becoming a safe place for myself."* Repeating these affirmations, especially when you feel anxious, reinforces a sense of safety and worthiness over time.

These exercises are small but mighty tools to reconnect with the younger parts of you that need healing. The more you incorporate these practices, the more you're building a sense of safety, compassion, and worthiness within yourself. And as you nurture this bond with your inner child, you're giving yourself the foundation to experience more secure, loving relationships in your life. Remember, every step toward healing your inner child is a gift that your present self—and all your future relationships—will thank you for.

PART 3: BUILDING CONFIDENCE AND EMOTIONAL SECURITY

CHAPTER 7: REWIRING YOUR ATTACHMENT PATTERNS

From Anxious to Secure Attachment

Imagine being able to step into a relationship with a calm heart, feeling secure in your worth, and trusting that you are enough just as you are. Moving from anxious to secure attachment is the journey toward this peace. And while it may sound challenging, remember, you're not alone in this process, and it doesn't require you to be "perfect" to work. With a mix of awareness, small shifts in behavior, and consistent practice, you'll begin to notice changes that bring you closer to secure attachment.

1. Recognize and Redirect Your Triggers

The first step to changing your attachment patterns is to become aware of what typically triggers your anxiety. Does it flare up when you don't get a response to a text right away? Or maybe when a partner is busy, and you're left wondering if they care as much as you do? Knowing these triggers allows you to interrupt the cycle before it spins out of control. Instead of spiraling into fear, try asking yourself: "What evidence do I have that I am safe and valued?" Shifting your focus away from fear-based assumptions to a balanced view gives your mind a much-needed break from anxious thought loops.

2. Practice Self-Soothing in the Moment

When you feel attachment anxiety kicking in, finding a way to self-soothe is essential. This could mean taking a few deep breaths, grounding yourself by focusing on something around you, or repeating an affirmation like, "I am secure, I am enough." It might feel awkward at first, but self-soothing teaches your brain that it doesn't need to rely on someone else to feel safe. You're reinforcing that you can give yourself calm and security from within.

3. Develop New Beliefs About Yourself and Relationships

Shifting attachment styles involves rewriting some core beliefs. Many people with anxious attachment have underlying beliefs like, "I am not lovable unless someone validates me," or, "If I'm not perfect, I'll be abandoned." Start working on replacing these old beliefs with new ones that reflect your worth and independence. Tell yourself things like, "I am valuable and deserving of love just as I am," or, "It's okay to take up space and have needs in a relationship." By creating a set of beliefs that come from a place of self-worth, you'll gradually feel less dependent on external validation.

4. Approach Relationships with Curiosity, Not Control

When anxious attachment patterns show up, it's easy to feel the need to control situations and outcomes—whether that's through checking in constantly, seeking reassurance, or even testing the other person's commitment. Instead, try approaching the relationship with curiosity. For example, instead of interpreting a delayed text as a sign of disinterest, ask yourself, "What else could be going on?" This shift helps you relax into the moment, making it easier to trust that your partner's behavior isn't a reflection of your worth.

5. Build a Foundation of Security in All Areas of Your Life

Moving toward secure attachment is about more than romantic relationships—it's about feeling secure in all aspects of your life. Cultivate a sense of independence by focusing on what makes you feel whole outside of a relationship. This could mean nurturing hobbies, building friendships, or developing your career. When you feel good about yourself in multiple areas, you become less likely to rely on a single relationship to fulfill all your needs, helping reduce anxiety and build a stronger foundation of self-worth.

6. Celebrate Small Wins

As you work on shifting from anxious to secure attachment, remember to acknowledge and celebrate your progress. Maybe you paused to breathe instead of reacting out of fear, or you waited to reply to a text without panicking. These small wins are milestones on your journey, building toward a more secure and empowered you.

Transitioning from anxious to secure attachment doesn't happen overnight, but with time and compassion for yourself, you'll get there. And each step you take not only strengthens your relationships but also brings you closer to a place of lasting inner peace.

ExercisesTop of Form

Changing deep-seated beliefs can feel like an uphill journey, especially when they've been there since childhood or formed from past relationships. But just as these beliefs were learned, they can be unlearned, too. This section introduces exercises designed to help you gently but effectively challenge and replace beliefs that keep you in a loop of anxiety, fear, or insecurity. These exercises are tools to build a new mental foundation, one rooted in confidence, resilience, and self-love.

1. Belief-Check Journal

Objective: To uncover and question limiting beliefs that contribute to anxious attachment.

Instructions: For one week, jot down moments when you feel anxious, insecure, or fearful in your relationship or when thinking about love in general. Beside each entry, write down any thoughts or beliefs that came up. For example, "If they're too busy to reply, they must not care about me." Once you've written it down, ask yourself:

- What evidence supports this belief?
- What evidence challenges this belief?
- What's a more balanced or supportive way to view this?
- This practice helps you see the difference between thoughts and facts, allowing you to soften the grip of anxious beliefs.

2. The Reframe and Replace Technique

Objective: To actively replace unhelpful beliefs with supportive, self-affirming ones.

Instructions: Write down one or two beliefs you recognize as unhelpful, like "I'm only lovable if I'm perfect" or "I'll be abandoned if I show my true self." For each belief, brainstorm a counter-belief that's realistic and affirming, such as "I am lovable for who I am, not what I do," or "Authenticity attracts the right people." When the unhelpful belief surfaces, repeat the replacement belief to yourself. You may not feel it immediately, but over time, your mind will start to accept these more supportive truths.

3. Evidence of Worth Exercise

Objective: To reinforce your sense of value and worth outside of your relationships.

Instructions: Every day for a week, write down three things that showcase your worth outside of your relationships. This could be a talent, a value you live by, an accomplishment, or a quality you appreciate about yourself. For example, "I'm good at making people feel heard," or "I handled a difficult task at work." At the end of the week, read over your list. These entries serve as reminders that your worth exists independently, reinforcing a secure sense of self.

4. Visualize Your Secure Self

Objective: To create a mental image of yourself acting from a place of secure attachment.

Instructions: Close your eyes and picture yourself in a relationship as a securely attached partner. Imagine how you would think, feel, and act. See yourself calm and confident, even if your partner is busy or dealing with their own issues. Picture yourself communicating openly, setting boundaries, and not second-guessing your worth.

Revisit this image whenever you feel anxious. Visualization can help retrain your mind to see this confident, secure self as your true self.

5. Practicing Self-Compassion Statements

Objective: To nurture self-acceptance and kindness, countering critical or anxious beliefs.

Instructions: When self-doubt creeps in, respond to it with a compassionate statement as if you were talking to a close friend. For instance, if you feel like you've made a mistake, instead of thinking "I always mess things up," you could say, "Everyone makes mistakes; this doesn't define my worth." Practice these compassionate responses regularly to build a kinder inner voice. Working with these exercises may feel uncomfortable at first, but remember, shifting beliefs is a gradual process. Each exercise you engage in is a step towards a more secure, loving relationship with yourself—and a more stable connection with others.

Shifting from Fear-Driven Reactions to Calm, Confident Responses

Picture this: Your partner doesn't reply to a message for hours, or you notice a change in their tone, and suddenly, fear takes over. Your mind races through worst-case scenarios, and before you know it, you're reacting—maybe with a text that sounds a bit too anxious, or a question that's too probing. It's not that you want to respond this way; it's just that your mind goes into overdrive, and fear does the driving.

The good news? You don't have to stay in this cycle. In this section, we'll explore ways to calm that initial fear response and replace it with grounded, confident reactions that reflect the real, resilient you. It's about learning how to hit pause on the fear and tune into a place of security, even when uncertainty looms.

1. Recognize the Trigger Moment

The first step is simple but powerful: notice when a situation starts triggering those fear-driven reactions. If your pulse quickens, your mind races, or you feel the urge to act immediately, these are signs that fear has taken the wheel. Acknowledging this in the moment gives you the chance to step back before fear can fully take over. A simple mental note, like "This is fear speaking," can be enough to break the cycle.

2. Pause and Breathe

When you're in a moment of fear, take a deep breath—a real one, that fills your lungs completely. This simple act can disrupt the fear spiral by giving your mind and body a moment to settle. Breathe in slowly for four counts, hold for two, and exhale for six. Repeat this a few times until you feel a slight release. You'd be amazed how much clarity and calmness just a few deep breaths can bring.

3. Question the Fear

Fear-driven reactions often stem from assumptions rather than facts. When you feel that anxious tug, ask yourself a few grounding questions:

- What evidence do I actually have right now?
- Could there be another explanation for this situation?
- Is this about my partner's behavior, or is it an old fear resurfacing?
- These questions don't deny your feelings but rather help you reframe the situation. They remind you to look at the broader picture, giving you room to respond from a place of calm rather than panic.

4. Rehearse Your Calm, Confident Self

Imagine yourself responding with confidence rather than anxiety. For example, if you're feeling the urge to double-text because your partner hasn't replied, visualize a version of yourself who's okay with waiting, who trusts that everything is fine. Picture this calm, confident self in detail—what you'd say, how you'd feel, how you'd handle the situation without rushing to soothe your fear. This exercise is like building a mental muscle; with practice, it becomes easier to embody that calm self in real time.

5. Embrace a Mantra for Stability

Sometimes, a simple mantra can anchor you when fear tries to creep in. Choose a phrase that feels reassuring, something like "I am secure and capable," or "I trust my ability to handle whatever comes." Repeat it when you start feeling anxious, using it as a touchstone to remind yourself that you're steady, resilient, and capable of calm responses.

6. Give Yourself Time to Respond

When fear-driven reactions arise, there's often an urge to respond instantly to alleviate the discomfort. But immediate reactions rarely come from a place of security. If you can, give yourself a little time—say, half an hour—to sit with the feelings before acting on them. Use this time to engage in a calming activity, like listening to a favorite song, going for a short walk, or practicing a hobby. By creating this buffer, you give your mind space to settle, allowing you to respond in a way that truly reflects your secure, confident self.

Shifting from fear-driven reactions to calm, confident responses is not about ignoring your feelings or pretending everything's perfect.

It's about learning to give yourself the security that anxious attachment may have deprived you of in the past. And with every instance where you practice this, you're reinforcing the truth that you're capable of feeling secure, of finding calm, and of responding from a place of confidence. This shift takes practice, but each small step adds up, strengthening your ability to show up as the most resilient, grounded version of yourself in any relationship.

CHAPTER 8: BUILDING SELF-WORTH AND INNER CONFIDENCE

Secure Sense of Self

Let's start with the heart of it all: building a secure, unshakable sense of self. When we feel secure within ourselves, we become less reliant on external validation, and our relationships become stronger, healthier, and less clouded by anxiety. This sense of self-worth can feel elusive, especially if you've spent years wrestling with feelings of insecurity or self-doubt. But here's the truth—it's entirely within your reach, and it starts with shifting how you see and talk to yourself every single day.

Understanding Your Core Worth

The first step in cultivating a secure sense of self is understanding that your worth isn't conditional. It doesn't hinge on someone else's approval, love, or opinion. This might feel hard to grasp, especially if you're used to looking to others for reassurance. But it's essential to recognize that your worth is inherent—it's there regardless of any relationship or external circumstance. You have value simply because you exist, and your unique experiences, insights, and strengths are what make you, you.

Recognizing Your Strengths and Unique Qualities

Take a moment to think about what you bring to the table—your qualities, skills, and strengths. What do others appreciate about you? What are you proud of, even if you rarely acknowledge it out loud? These might be things as simple as your listening skills, your empathy, or your ability to make others laugh. Write these down and revisit them regularly. This list serves as a reminder of who you are at your core—a foundation of strengths and positive traits that contribute to your unique sense of self.

Silencing the Inner Critic

Most of us have a critical voice in our heads that constantly questions our worth, particularly when we're feeling vulnerable or insecure. This voice may point out flaws, amplify insecurities, or compare us to others. To cultivate a secure sense of self, it's crucial to recognize when this critic is speaking up and learn how to manage it. Remember, you are not your inner critic—this voice might reflect past fears or doubts, but it doesn't define you. Try responding to this voice with compassion instead of feeding its negative energy. Say to yourself, "I hear you, but I know my worth, and I am choosing to believe in myself."

Building Self-Trust

Self-worth and confidence grow stronger when you can trust yourself. Self-trust means knowing that you have your own back, that you can make choices aligned with your well-being, and that you'll be okay, regardless of what happens. Building self-trust takes time, but it starts with small steps. It might look like keeping a promise to yourself to take time each day to relax, listening to your intuition in deciding, or speaking up about how you feel in a safe setting. Each time you trust yourself, you reinforce the message that you're capable, reliable, and secure.

Embracing Self-Compassion

Let's face it: everyone has days when self-worth feels like a bit of a struggle. When you encounter these moments, practice self-compassion. Imagine how you'd speak to a dear friend who's feeling low and offer that same warmth to yourself. Remind yourself that it's okay to have setbacks; it doesn't diminish your value. Self-compassion isn't just about being kind to yourself—it's a powerful way of acknowledging that you're worthy of love and understanding, even when things aren't perfect.

Setting Intentions Aligned with Your True Self

Finally, a secure sense of self is about living authentically, which means acting in ways that feel true to who you are, not who you think you should be to please others. Setting intentions that reflect your genuine interests, goals, and values is an act of self-respect. Ask yourself what truly matters to you and start aligning your choices with those priorities. Each step toward living authentically solidifies your self-worth, as you're honoring your unique path.

Building a secure sense of self is not about transforming into someone else or meeting a set of impossible standards. Instead, it's about discovering and cherishing the person you already are. With time, these steps become part of your daily routine, and bit by bit, you'll notice a deep sense of self-assurance taking root. This confidence radiates beyond relationships, enriching every part of your life. Because when you're secure in yourself, you're able to show up fully in your connections, no longer weighed down by doubt or fear. And that's the version of you the world is waiting to see.

Detaching Your Self-Worth from Outcomes

It's easy to fall into the trap of equating relationship success with our own self-worth. Many of us have felt that if a relationship is going well, we must be doing something right. But if it's rocky, or if someone decides to leave, we immediately start questioning our own value. Learning to detach your self-worth from relationship outcomes is a game-changer—it frees you from the emotional rollercoaster of tying your worth to someone else's actions or decisions.

Understanding the Difference Between Connection and Validation

One of the most crucial steps here is understanding that the love and connection you experience in a relationship are beautiful, but they don't define your core value. Relationships can bring us joy, comfort, and even a sense of purpose, but they're only one part of who we are. When you can see relationships as enriching rather than defining, you begin to recognize that your worth doesn't fluctuate based on someone else's behavior or feelings toward you.

Refocusing on Your Inner Sense of Value

The real work of self-worth happens internally. It's about seeing yourself clearly, celebrating your qualities, and respecting your boundaries regardless of your relationship status. Take a moment to reflect on who you are outside of relationships—what makes you unique, resilient, and lovable? Reaffirming this to yourself regularly can keep you grounded. That inner stability helps you approach relationships with openness, not fear, because you're no longer relying on them to prove your worth.

Navigating Challenges Without Self-Blame

Relationships can be challenging, and conflicts will come up—that's normal. But detaching your self-worth means learning to approach these bumps without letting them affect your sense of self. If things go wrong, it's not necessarily a reflection of your worth. Everyone has their own journey and personal struggles, and sometimes, those don't align with ours. Recognize that challenges don't make you "less than"; instead, they offer a chance to grow and understand yourself better.

Letting Go of People-Pleasing Habits

When our self-worth feels tied to relationships, people-pleasing often creeps in. You might find yourself putting others' needs before your own or feeling anxious about keeping everyone happy. But this habit can leave you feeling drained and disconnected from your authentic self. Practice speaking up about your needs and setting boundaries, even if it feels uncomfortable. It's okay to want a healthy, balanced relationship that doesn't require sacrificing your well-being.

Embracing Self-Worth as a Constant

Your worth is steady, independent of who you're with, whether a relationship succeeds or falters. Imagine it as a solid foundation that's unshaken by external events. The beauty of this mindset is that it allows you to show up in relationships from a place of wholeness. You're not seeking validation or acceptance; you're simply bringing your full, true self to the connection. And in doing so, you attract people who appreciate and respect that.

Learning to separate your self-worth from relationship outcomes takes time, but it's deeply empowering. As you practice this, you'll start to feel a sense of inner freedom—a release from the pressure to "perform" in relationships or prove your worth through someone else's approval. You're worthy just as you are, and that's a truth no relationship can change. Holding onto that belief makes all the difference, allowing you to approach love with confidence, not fear.

Mindfulness Practices

Building emotional resilience can sometimes feel like a challenge, especially when relationships stir up anxiety, insecurities, or self-doubt. But there's a powerful tool available to you right here, right now—mindfulness. Through simple, daily practices, mindfulness helps you reconnect with yourself, find peace amidst chaos, and build the resilience you need to face life's ups and downs.

Learning to Stay Present

One of the hardest things about anxious attachment is that our minds often get stuck in a cycle of worry: "What if they leave?" "What did that last text mean?" "Do they still care about me?" Mindfulness teaches us how to come back to the present, to stop wandering into a future we can't control. By grounding ourselves in what's happening right now, we ease our fears and bring clarity to our emotions. Take just a few moments each day to observe your breathing. Let each inhale and exhale remind you that you're safe in this moment.

Observing Your Emotions Without Judgment

Mindfulness isn't about suppressing emotions; it's about noticing them without letting them take control. Instead of fighting feelings of fear, jealousy, or insecurity, try to observe them. Imagine you're watching clouds drift by in the sky—sometimes they're dark and heavy, sometimes light and fluffy. Your emotions are like those clouds. They come and go, but they don't define the sky. By learning to observe rather than react, you build resilience and see that no feeling is permanent.

Cultivating Self-Compassion

Resilience isn't just about being tough; it's about being kind to yourself, especially on the hard days. Mindfulness encourages self-compassion. When you're feeling vulnerable or anxious, talk to yourself the way you would comfort a friend. Remind yourself that it's okay to struggle, and that healing takes time. Little by little, this self-kindness becomes a part of your routine, giving you the inner strength to face whatever comes.

Daily Practices to Build Resilience

Consider adding small mindful rituals into your day. You might start your morning with a few minutes of deep breathing, setting a calm tone for the day. During meals, try eating slowly and savoring each bite, allowing yourself to be fully present. At the end of the day, write down three things you're grateful for—big or small. Over time, these moments of mindfulness build a habit of inner calm, helping you return to yourself in moments of stress.

Using Mindfulness to Respond Instead of React

Emotional resilience grows when we learn to respond thoughtfully rather than react impulsively. Instead of immediately texting back out of anxiety, pause and ask yourself, "What do I really want to communicate?" or "How do I want to feel after this?" These small pauses—mindful moments—allow you to choose calm over worry, clarity over confusion. Each time you respond from a place of mindfulness, you build a foundation of resilience, proving to yourself that you can handle difficult emotions.

A Gentle Path Forward

Mindfulness is an ongoing practice, not a quick fix. It's the gentle yet powerful approach that builds resilience from within. As you commit to these small practices, you'll notice subtle shifts—a calm that stays with you a little longer, a sense of self-trust that grows a bit stronger. And this resilience, rooted in mindfulness, becomes your steady anchor, grounding you through every twist and turn. It's not about achieving "perfect calm," but about showing up each day for yourself, knowing that you're capable of handling whatever comes your way.

CHAPTER 9: SETTING HEALTHY BOUNDARIES

The Importance of Boundaries

Creating boundaries in relationships can feel a little daunting, especially when we're worried about pushing someone away or risking conflict. But here's a powerful truth: boundaries aren't walls designed to keep others out; they're bridges that allow healthier, more secure connections. Boundaries are the foundation of emotional safety, allowing us to protect our well-being and communicate clearly about our needs.

Boundaries are essential because they remind us of what's okay and what isn't—both for us and the people we care about. Think of a boundary like a gentle reminder that says, "I value myself and our relationship enough to show up authentically." Without boundaries, we can start feeling resentful, overwhelmed, or even taken for granted. In fact, without clear boundaries, it's easy to become anxious, as if we're responsible for managing every little detail in a relationship. Setting boundaries offers the emotional safety to be ourselves, which is a gift to us and our relationships.

Protecting Your Well-being with Boundaries

When we don't set boundaries, we risk our mental and emotional health by allowing too much into our personal space—demands, expectations, or behaviors that leave us feeling drained. Boundaries provide the buffer we need to feel safe and centered. They allow us to let in the positive while filtering out what isn't serving our growth. And when we do this, we can approach our relationships with more generosity and energy, knowing we're taking care of ourselves first.

Boundaries as Expressions of Respect

Boundaries are a way to show respect—both for us and others. By creating and respecting boundaries, we show that we're willing to communicate openly and honestly, which ultimately strengthens trust. When we're clear about what we need, we give our partners, friends, or family the chance to understand us more deeply. They know where we stand, and we give them the chance to respond authentically.

Building the Foundation for Secure Attachment

For those with anxious attachment tendencies, setting boundaries can be an important step toward a more secure, trusting relationship. Establishing healthy limits allows us to feel less anxious because we're no longer overextending ourselves or constantly second-guessing how much to give. Instead, we learn that we can protect our emotional safety without the fear of losing connection. This act of boundary-setting builds a healthier, more balanced dynamic, where both people feel valued and respected.

So, as we explore setting and communicating boundaries, remember this: boundaries aren't about shutting people out—they're about inviting them in, on terms that honor both their needs and yours. They are a powerful tool that allows you to be fully present and at ease in your relationships, providing the peace of mind that comes from emotional safety.

How to assert your needs

Expressing your needs assertively might feel unfamiliar—especially if you've spent years prioritizing others' comfort over your own. But here's the truth: healthy relationships flourish when both people feel free to express their needs openly. When you voice what's important to you, you're giving others the chance to understand and respond with care. This isn't about demanding; it's about inviting genuine connection and understanding.

Why Assertive Communication Matters

Assertive communication is like putting a compass on the table in any relationship. It says, "This is the direction that feels right for me," which is incredibly helpful for both you and the other person.

It's about being honest, transparent, and clear about what matters to you. When you start sharing your needs confidently and calmly, you invite a response that's authentic—because now everyone knows what page you're on.

Steps to Communicate Assertively

- Start with "I" Statements

Using "I" statements shifts the conversation away from blame or accusations and grounds it in your own experience. Saying, "I feel anxious when we don't communicate regularly" instead of "You never keep in touch" is much more likely to lead to an open and supportive response.

- Be Clear and Specific

Vague hints or hoping someone will "just understand" often lead to misunderstandings or disappointment. Instead, be as specific as possible. If you feel more secure with regular check-ins, say, "I feel most connected and valued when we check in with each other each day."

- Keep the Tone Calm and Open

Assertive communication isn't about confrontation. Try to enter the conversation with a calm, open tone. Think of it as inviting a friend to see a glimpse of your inner world—how you experience things and what makes you feel safe and happy. Keeping a gentle approach can ease the conversation and help the other person feel more at ease too.

- Acknowledge Your Emotions without Apology

You don't need to apologize for what you need. It's natural to feel a twinge of worry about coming off as "too much" or "too needy," but remind yourself that expressing your needs is simply a part of healthy communication. Instead of, "I'm sorry, but I need to ask for…" you could say, "I'd like to share something important for me to feel safe and supported in our relationship."

- Prepare for a Range of Reactions

Asserting your needs may be new for those around you, and they might need time to adjust. Remember, the goal isn't necessarily to have everyone agree immediately. It's about starting the habit of expressing your needs in a way that feels authentic to you. You're opening the door to mutual understanding, which is worth any initial discomfort.

- Reflect and Adjust Over Time

After you share your needs, give yourself a moment to reflect on how it felt. Did you feel heard and respected? Adjust your approach as needed to make this practice more comfortable and aligned with who you are.

Each time you communicate your needs, you're building a foundation of confidence and respect. You're honoring yourself, and with each attempt, it becomes a little easier to show up as the whole, valued person you are. Assertive communication isn't a one-time skill—it's a practice that grows stronger each time you give yourself permission to be open and clear.

Setting limits without fear

Setting limits can feel daunting, especially when you fear rejection. It's entirely normal to worry about how others will react when you assert your boundaries. You might find yourself second-guessing whether your needs are valid or whether you're being "too demanding." But here's the essential truth: your boundaries are a crucial part of your emotional well-being and help foster healthier, more fulfilling relationships.

Understanding the Fear of Rejection

Many of us have a deep-rooted fear of rejection that stems from our desire for connection and belonging. This fear can be especially pronounced for those with anxious attachment styles, who may equate setting boundaries with jeopardizing their relationships. You might worry that if you say "no" or express a need, you'll push someone away or risk their love and acceptance.

But let's reframe that thought setting limits doesn't have to mean losing connection; it can strengthen it. When you clearly define what's acceptable and what's not, you're not only taking care of yourself but also teaching others how to treat you. This is a powerful act of self-love and respect.

Strategies for Setting Limits Without Fear

- Recognize Your Right to Set Boundaries

First and foremost, understand that it's your right to set limits. Everyone has different needs, and honoring yours doesn't take away from anyone else's. Accepting this truth is the first step toward freeing yourself from the fear of rejection.

- Communicate with Compassion

When you approach boundary-setting, frame it with compassion and empathy. Use language that reflects your desire for understanding, not conflict. For example, you could say, "I really value our time together, but I need a little space to recharge right now." This shows you care about the relationship while also asserting your needs.

- Practice Self-Validation

Before you express your limits, remind yourself that your feelings and needs are valid. Engage in positive self-talk to build your confidence. Saying things like, "It's okay for me to need time alone" or "I deserve to express my needs" can empower you before having a conversation.

- Prepare for Possible Reactions

Understand that not everyone will react positively, and that's okay. Some people might be surprised, while others may need time to adjust. Prepare for this by acknowledging that their initial discomfort doesn't reflect your worth or the value of your needs.

- Use "I" Statements

"I" statements are powerful tools for expressing your feelings and needs without placing blame. For example, say, "I feel overwhelmed when I don't have time to myself" instead of "You always take up my time." This method helps to keep the focus on your experience rather than making the other person defensive.

- Stay Firm Yet Flexible

When you set a boundary, be firm in your stance while remaining open to conversation. If the other person expresses concern or confusion, listen to them. Flexibility can lead to mutual understanding but be careful not to compromise your core limits just to avoid discomfort.

- Celebrate Small Wins

Acknowledge your courage each time you set a limit, no matter how small. Celebrate your progress, whether it's successfully communicating your need for alone time or standing your ground in a challenging conversation. Each step forward reinforces your confidence and reminds you of your strength.

Embracing the Freedom of Boundaries

Remember, setting limits is not a barrier to love and connection; it's a bridge to deeper understanding and respect. When you communicate your boundaries openly, you create space for more honest and fulfilling relationships. Your true self shines brighter when you're not weighed down by the fear of rejection.

By embracing the process of boundary-setting, you're stepping into a more empowered version of yourself—one who knows their worth and stands firmly in it. The more you practice this skill, the more natural it will become, leading to stronger, healthier connections in your life.

PART 4: FOSTERING SECURE AND LOVING RELATIONSHIPS

CHAPTER 10: BUILDING TRUST AND EMOTIONAL INTIMACY

Building trust after a history of insecurity can feel like an uphill journey. If you've been through relationships where trust was shaky or inconsistent, it's natural to feel a bit guarded now. But fostering trust—especially when it hasn't come easily in the past—is a skill you can build, one that grows stronger with intention, patience, and the right actions.

Why It Matters

Trust forms the foundation of every healthy, secure relationship. It allows us to feel safe, open, and connected. Without trust, it's difficult to relax or feel fully comfortable being ourselves with someone else. Trust is what transforms a connection from surface-level to deep, honest, and lasting.

Rebuilding Trust in Yourself

Before we even look at fostering trust with others, let's focus on building trust in yourself. This is essential because if you're constantly doubting your own worth, judgment, or choices, trusting someone else becomes even harder. To start:

Practice Self-Honesty: Be open with yourself about your feelings, needs, and fears. Self-honesty means acknowledging what you truly want, even if it's uncomfortable or challenging. When you know you can trust yourself to face your own feelings, it's easier to be transparent with others.

Honor Your Own Boundaries: Show yourself that you're committed to protecting your well-being by setting and respecting boundaries. This practice builds self-respect, which is a crucial component of self-trust.

Follow Through on Small Promises to Yourself: When you make commitments to yourself—like taking time for self-care, pursuing a personal goal, or simply giving yourself a break—follow through. This reinforces your sense of self-reliability, which is foundational for feeling confident in relationships.

Creating a Trustworthy Environment with Your Partner
Now, when it comes to fostering trust in a relationship, creating a reliable and supportive environment is key. Think of this as the structure that allows trust to grow over time:

Show Consistency: Trust grows when words and actions align consistently over time. Try to communicate openly and follow through on your commitments. It's okay if you're not perfect—no one is—but consistency in the small things, like being reliable and keeping your word, goes a long way.

Be Transparent with Your Partner: Share your thoughts, feelings, and experiences openly. Letting someone see your true self, flaws and all, builds closeness and authenticity. Vulnerability is a powerful way to foster trust because it signals that you're willing to let them see you, even when you feel vulnerable.

Listen with Empathy: Trust is a two-way street, and it's crucial to show your partner that they can trust you, too. Practice listening without judgment or jumping in with advice. Often, just being there for someone as they share their thoughts can be one of the most trust-building things you can do.

How to Navigate Moments of Doubt

If you're working to rebuild trust, doubts and insecurities may pop up, and that's completely normal. Here are some ways to manage those moments without letting them erode your connection:

Pause and Reflect: When doubts arise, take a pause. Check in with yourself about where they're coming from. Are they based on past experiences, or something happening in the present? Reflection helps you distinguish between real concerns and old patterns.

Communicate Your Feelings Calmly: If something in your relationship sparks insecurity, try to bring it up in a way that's constructive. Instead of accusing or blaming, share how you feel and what you need to feel more secure. For example, saying, "When plans change last minute, I feel uneasy. Can we talk about how we could handle that differently?" helps build understanding.

Focus on Building Positive Experiences Together: Take small steps to create shared memories and positive moments with your partner. Whether it's a weekly activity you both enjoy, open conversations, or little acts of kindness, every positive experience adds to the foundation of trust.

Trust as a Journey

Remember, building trust—whether in yourself or with someone else—is not an instant process. It's a gradual journey that unfolds one step, one choice, one honest conversation at a time. And each time you choose to trust (even just a little), you're showing yourself that secure, loving relationships are possible.

So be patient and kind to yourself along the way. With every effort you put into this process, you're creating a safe space for both you and your partner to feel valued, respected, and genuinely connected.

Emotional intimacy

Emotional intimacy is the magic that turns a relationship from simply functional to deeply meaningful. It's about more than just sharing space or spending time together—it's the feeling of truly being seen, understood, and accepted by another person. For many of us, this kind of connection is the ultimate goal in a relationship. But nurturing it, especially if you're not used to it or if past experiences have made you cautious, can feel daunting. Let's break down what emotional intimacy really means and explore ways to cultivate it.

What is Emotional Intimacy?

At its core, emotional intimacy is the sense that you and your partner are safe to be yourselves, without fear of judgment or rejection. It's about sharing your inner world—your thoughts, fears, hopes, and dreams—and knowing that your partner respects and values those things, even if they don't always understand or agree with them. Emotional intimacy makes it possible to be vulnerable without feeling exposed or insecure.

A common misconception is that emotional intimacy just "happens." While chemistry and compatibility play a role, intimacy requires nurturing, honesty, and commitment from both partners. It's the ongoing choice to be open, present, and supportive, even when it's challenging.

How to Nurture Emotional Intimacy

Be Curious and Attentive: One of the simplest but most powerful ways to nurture intimacy is by genuinely listening to your partner. Show interest in their day, ask questions, and pay attention to the little things they share. This shows that you care about their experiences and value their perspective. It can be as simple as asking, "How did that make you feel?" or "What's been on your mind lately?"

Share Your Inner World: Emotional intimacy is a two-way street. While it feels wonderful when your partner opens up to you, they need to feel that same trust and closeness. Don't be afraid to let them in on what you're thinking and feeling—even if it's something small or something you're hesitant to admit. Saying things like, "I felt a bit insecure today because…" or "This is something I'm really excited about" lets them feel closer to you.

Express Appreciation Regularly: Let your partner know when they've done something that makes you feel loved, appreciated, or understood. Small moments of acknowledgment—whether it's for making you laugh, helping with a task, or just being there—create a positive emotional space in the relationship. It reinforces the bond and helps build a foundation where both of you feel valued.

Be Present, Not Just Physically but Emotionally: Presence is about more than just being in the same room. It's about making a conscious effort to focus on each other without distractions. In our busy lives, it can be tempting to multitask or let our minds wander, but taking intentional time to truly be present—whether that's over dinner, during a walk, or even just sitting together—gives both of you space to feel connected.

Allow Vulnerability to Show: Vulnerability is the key to emotional intimacy, but it's not always easy to let someone see our fears, insecurities, or past hurts. You might worry about how your partner will respond, or if they'll truly understand. But letting them in, even if it's just little by little, creates a powerful sense of trust. It tells your partner, "I trust you with this part of me," which deepens your bond.

Respect Each Other's Boundaries and Differences: Emotional intimacy also means respecting that you and your partner are different people, with unique needs, boundaries, and viewpoints. Part of nurturing closeness is learning where your partner's comfort zones are and respecting them, even as you work to grow together. This respect builds a sense of safety and trust that ultimately strengthens your connection.

Work Through Conflicts with Empathy and Openness: Disagreements are inevitable, but they don't have to drive you apart. In fact, resolving conflicts in a healthy way often brings people closer together. When conflicts arise, try to approach them with empathy, staying focused on understanding each other rather than "winning" the argument. Practice patience and look for solutions together.

Making Emotional Intimacy a Habit

Building and sustaining emotional intimacy takes time, but small, consistent efforts are often all it takes. Checking in with each other, sharing something new about yourself, or finding ways to support your partner on a regular basis can all go a long way. If either of you ever feels that intimacy is slipping, that's okay too. Just bringing it up gently can help you both get back on track.

Remember, emotional intimacy isn't about perfection; it's about presence. It's the joy of knowing that, at the end of the day, you have someone who truly knows you—and you know them. As you nurture this closeness, you're creating a relationship built on trust, acceptance, and genuine connection.

Deepening connection

Deepening your connection with your partner isn't just about the big gestures or perfect dates; it's about the small, meaningful actions that remind both of you that you're in this together. Relationships thrive when both people feel valued, understood, and connected on a deeper level. Let's explore some practical, powerful ways to make your bond even stronger.

1. Make Time for Each Other Regularly

Life gets busy, and it's easy to push quality time to the side. But setting aside dedicated time for each other—even if it's just 15 minutes a day—can have a huge impact. This could be something as simple as enjoying a morning coffee together, taking a short walk after dinner, or having a regular "unplugged" night where you both put away phones and just talk or share a quiet activity. This consistency builds a foundation of connection that grows over time.

2. Show Appreciation Often

When you express gratitude for each other's actions—both big and small—you're reinforcing the bond between you. Did your partner pick up groceries, make you laugh, or just give you a warm smile when you needed it? Saying "thank you" or acknowledging these moments, even in passing, makes them feel valued. You might be surprised at how powerful it is to feel seen and appreciated every day.

3. Create Rituals or Special Traditions

Little rituals can become touchstones in your relationship, giving you both something special to look forward to. Maybe it's a weekly movie night, a Saturday breakfast tradition, or writing each other a short note on anniversaries. These moments don't have to be elaborate; they just need to be yours. By establishing these rituals, you're creating lasting memories and reinforcing your connection.

4. Be Curious About Each Other's Inner Worlds

Even if you've been together for years, there's always more to discover about each other. Make it a habit to ask open-ended questions—about each other's dreams, fears, current challenges, or what's bringing them joy right now. Genuine curiosity shows that you're interested in who your partner is today, not just who they were when you first met. This openness helps you stay connected as you both grow and change over time.

5. Offer Unconditional Support During Tough Times

Life's challenges, big and small, can sometimes feel overwhelming. When your partner is going through something hard, being there for them without judgment or trying to "fix" things can mean the world. Listen, offer comfort, and let them know they don't have to face it alone. This support not only helps them feel secure, but also deepens your emotional connection. The knowledge that they can count on you through thick and thin creates an unshakable foundation of trust.

6. Show Physical Affection Regularly

Physical touch is a powerful way to feel connected, and it doesn't always have to be romantic or intimate in nature. Small gestures—a hand squeeze, a hug, a gentle touch on the shoulder—can remind your partner that you're there and that you care. If physical affection is meaningful to both of you, make it a regular part of your day, as it can enhance feelings of security and closeness.

7. Practice Active Listening

When your partner is sharing something with you, whether it's a major concern or a minor story, make an effort to be fully present. Nod, ask follow-up questions, and respond to show that you're listening. Avoid interrupting or jumping in with your own story. Active listening demonstrates respect and helps your partner feel truly heard, which can go a long way in building trust and intimacy.

8. Work on Forgiveness and Letting Go

All relationships face challenges and misunderstandings. The ability to forgive—to let go of hurt feelings or old arguments—helps both of you move forward without resentment. Holding onto grudges only keeps you both stuck, while forgiveness allows space for growth and healing. Remember, forgiveness isn't about forgetting; it's about valuing the relationship enough to look past mistakes and embrace each other fully, flaws and all.

9. Dream Together

Building a shared vision for the future can be incredibly bonding. Talk about your dreams, both individually and as a couple. Whether it's future travel plans, personal goals, or where you'd like to be in five years, discussing these aspirations gives you both something to look forward to and work toward together. Having shared goals fosters unity and a sense of purpose in your relationship.

10. Celebrate Each Other's Wins

Life's successes feel even sweeter when they're shared. Celebrate your partner's achievements, no matter how small. If they accomplish something meaningful to them, take a moment to acknowledge it, show your excitement, and celebrate together. When you take pride in each other's wins, it builds a sense of partnership and belonging that strengthens your connection.

Putting It All Together

Deepening your connection doesn't mean doing everything perfectly; it's about making an effort to stay close and show love, especially when it matters most. With each intentional act, you're investing in a relationship built on mutual respect, trust, and genuine care. By making these strategies part of your everyday life, you'll create a space where both of you feel deeply valued and supported— a relationship that's resilient, fulfilling, and beautifully secure.

CHAPTER 11: COMMUNICATING IN SECURE RELATIONSHIPS

Communicate without fear

Talking openly in relationships can feel vulnerable—especially when you've experienced a history of anxious attachment or fear of abandonment. It's only natural to worry about how your words might be received, or to wonder if expressing your true feelings could push your partner away. But learning to communicate without fear is a crucial step toward building a strong, secure, and healthy relationship. Let's explore what it means to communicate openly, without that underlying fear of rejection.

1. Understand That Your Feelings Are Valid

First and foremost, it's important to remind yourself that your feelings and thoughts matter. They're not a burden or something to be brushed aside. In a secure relationship, you and your partner both deserve to feel heard and understood. Recognize that expressing yourself isn't "too much" or "needy"—it's a natural and healthy part of connection. When you trust in the validity of your feelings, sharing them becomes a little easier.

2. Start with Small Vulnerabilities

If opening up fully feels intimidating, start with small things. Share something simple that's on your mind, like how your day went or a small worry you have. Practicing openness in little ways can build your confidence, creating a foundation of trust where you feel safer to share more personal feelings over time. Remember, vulnerability is something you can ease into; it doesn't have to happen all at once.

3. Choose a Calm Moment to Talk

Timing can make a big difference. When you're feeling anxious or triggered, your words might come out in ways you don't intend, or your partner may feel defensive. Instead, look for a calm, quiet moment to talk, when you're both in a relaxed mindset. Approaching these conversations from a place of calm can help them feel more constructive and reduce the likelihood of misunderstandings or reactive emotions.

4. Use "I" Statements to Take Ownership of Your Feelings

An "I" statement allows you to communicate in a way that centers on your experience, rather than sounding like a critique of your partner. For example, saying, "I feel worried when I don't hear from you" expresses how you feel without assigning blame. This kind of statement not only makes it easier for your partner to understand where you're coming from, but it also minimizes defensiveness and encourages empathy. By taking ownership of your emotions, you make the conversation less about blame and more about connection.

5. Check in with Yourself First

Before diving into a conversation, take a moment to ask yourself, "What am I really feeling?" and "What do I need right now?" Sometimes, fear of abandonment can make us feel heightened emotions, like anxiety or frustration, but underneath those might be feelings of loneliness or a need for reassurance. When you're clear about what you're truly experiencing, it's easier to communicate it clearly and authentically.

6. Trust in Your Partner's Capacity to Respond

One of the hardest parts of open communication is trusting that your partner can handle what you're sharing. It's natural to fear their reaction, but remind yourself that in a secure, loving relationship, your partner wants to know your inner world. Trust that they're capable of listening and responding with compassion. Even if their response isn't perfect, the act of sharing creates a foundation for understanding and closeness.

7. Let Go of the Need for a Perfect Outcome

We often put pressure on ourselves to have the "perfect" conversation or to say things in a way that guarantees a specific response. But when we communicate with a focus on controlling the outcome, it only adds to our anxiety. Instead, approach your conversations with the goal of sharing your truth, rather than trying to manage how it will be received. Trust that you're doing your part by being open, and allow the conversation to unfold naturally.

8. Celebrate Small Wins in Openness

Each time you open up—even if it feels uncomfortable at first—acknowledge your courage. Notice the positive impact it has, not only on your relationship but also on your self-esteem. Every time you share a piece of yourself, you're building resilience and reducing your fear of abandonment, step by step.

Embracing Open Communication as a Path to Security

Open, honest communication is like a muscle: the more you practice it, the stronger it becomes. Every time you face the fear of abandonment head-on and speak your truth, you're moving closer to a secure attachment style. This doesn't mean the fear will disappear overnight, but each time you choose honesty over silence, you're building trust with your partner and within yourself.

Remember, communication in a secure relationship isn't about being perfect or fearless—it's about showing up as your authentic self, trusting that your relationship can hold space for your feelings.

As you continue practicing, the fear of abandonment will lessen, replaced by a sense of calm confidence and the knowledge that you and your partner can navigate life's ups and downs together.

Conflict resolution

Conflict can be tough in any relationship, especially when feelings like jealousy and insecurity are involved. But here's the thing: conflict itself isn't a sign of a weak relationship; it's actually a natural part of every connection. When handled in a healthy way, conflict can even strengthen your bond. Learning how to work through it without letting jealousy or insecurity take the wheel is one of the most empowering steps you can take toward a secure, fulfilling relationship.

1. Understand That Conflict Isn't a Threat

When you have an anxious attachment style, it's easy to feel like every disagreement is a sign that something is deeply wrong. But conflict doesn't mean the relationship is at risk. It's simply two people with different perspectives and emotions navigating life together. Recognizing this can help you step into conflicts without that nagging fear of loss, which often fuels jealousy and insecurity.

2. Pause to Check Your Feelings

Before diving into the conflict, pause and ask yourself what you're really feeling. Is it anger, or is it fear of rejection? Is it jealousy, or is it insecurity about your own worth? When you get to the root of your feelings, you can approach the conversation from a place of clarity, rather than reacting impulsively. It also lets you speak to what's truly on your mind without letting insecurity cloud your words.

3. Practice Empathy, for Yourself and Your Partner

Remember that it's okay to feel jealous or insecure sometimes—it doesn't make you a "bad" partner. These feelings are part of being human. By acknowledging them, you're already halfway to resolving them. Then, try to see things from your partner's perspective, too. Practicing empathy doesn't mean ignoring your feelings; it means understanding that both of you have needs and emotions that deserve respect.

4. Use "I" Statements to Express Your Feelings

When talking about what's bothering you, try using "I" statements, like "I feel insecure when…" or "I need reassurance because…." This approach doesn't place blame on your partner, which reduces their defensiveness and makes it easier to discuss your feelings openly. By focusing on your own experience, you're inviting them to support you, rather than making them feel at fault.

5. Replace Assumptions with Curiosity

When we feel insecure or jealous, our minds often jump to conclusions, creating scenarios that feed our fears. Instead of assuming, try asking questions. For example, if you feel uneasy about your partner's friendship with someone, approach it with curiosity. Ask about their perspective, listen to their feelings, and share your own. This shifts the focus from confrontation to understanding and gives your partner a chance to offer reassurance.

6. Find Ways to Soothe Yourself in the Moment

Conflict can bring up strong emotions, and it's important to have tools to soothe yourself. Take a few deep breaths, go for a walk, or remind yourself of times when things worked out in your relationship. These small acts can help calm your mind, making it easier to approach the conflict without letting jealousy or insecurity take control.

7. Focus on Solutions, Not on Winning

Healthy conflict resolution isn't about proving who's right or wrong; it's about finding a path forward that feels good for both of you. Instead of seeing the conflict as a battle to be won, try viewing it as a shared problem to solve. Ask each other, "What can we both do to make this situation better?" This way, the conflict becomes a teamwork exercise rather than a standoff.

8. Reflect on Your Progress, Not Just the Outcome
Even if the conflict doesn't end in a perfect resolution, take a moment to recognize the effort you put into approaching it differently. Each time you choose empathy, communicate openly, or pause before reacting, you're strengthening your emotional resilience. Over time, these small steps add up, making jealousy and insecurity less and less of a factor in your conflicts.

Embracing Conflict as a Path to Growth
Healthy conflict resolution is about feeling secure enough to work through disagreements without letting jealousy and insecurity take over. Remember, every time you handle conflict in a new, constructive way, you're rewiring your attachment patterns and reinforcing your sense of security. Conflict then becomes less of a threat and more of an opportunity to build trust, deepen intimacy, and show up authentically.

You're not just learning to navigate conflict; you're learning to create a relationship where both of you feel safe, respected, and valued—even in the tough moments. This journey won't always be easy, but the peace and confidence you'll find in a healthier conflict dynamic are more than worth it.

Power of vulnerability

Vulnerability is one of the most powerful tools we have for building deep, meaningful connections. Yet, it can also feel terrifying—especially if you're someone who's faced insecurity or fear of rejection in past relationships. But vulnerability isn't about oversharing or putting yourself at unnecessary risk. Rather, it's about letting someone see the real you, allowing your authentic self to be seen, heard, and valued.

1. What Vulnerability Really Means

When we talk about vulnerability, it's easy to think it means exposing all your wounds, weaknesses, or insecurities to someone else. In reality, vulnerability is more about honesty and openness, about showing up as yourself without the masks we sometimes wear to feel safer. It's about letting your partner in on your hopes, fears, and dreams—even when it feels a little risky.

2. Why Vulnerability Builds Connection

Think about the times you've felt closest to someone. It's usually not because they were perfect; it's because they were real with you. They shared something personal or let you in on their world in a way that felt genuine. When you allow yourself to be vulnerable, you're giving your partner a chance to truly understand you—and, in turn, to be vulnerable with you. This mutual openness is the foundation of trust and emotional intimacy.

3. Overcoming the Fear of Being Seen

If you've struggled with anxious attachment, the fear of rejection can make being vulnerable feel like an emotional gamble. What if they pull away? What if they think less of you? These questions are normal, but vulnerability is about trusting that the right person will appreciate your honesty. Start small by sharing how certain things make you feel—express a fear, a hope, or a dream. With each step, you'll see that vulnerability doesn't drive people away; it draws them closer.

4. Using Vulnerability as a Tool for Emotional Growth

Being vulnerable doesn't just help your partner understand you better; it also helps you understand yourself. When you express your true feelings, you're facing them head-on, rather than letting them fester in the background. Over time, this practice helps you build a stronger, more confident sense of self. You'll begin to realize that your feelings are valid and worth sharing, and that this openness is a source of strength, not weakness.

5. How to Embrace Vulnerability in Everyday Life

Try bringing a little vulnerability into your daily interactions. It could be as simple as sharing your thoughts about something that happened during your day, or opening up about a small worry. Vulnerability isn't about having "big talks" all the time; it's about allowing your partner to experience your world. These moments of openness create a steady rhythm of trust that builds over time.

6. Accepting Your Partner's Vulnerability, Too

Being vulnerable goes both ways. As you share your own experiences, listen to and accept your partner's moments of vulnerability as well. Let them feel seen, heard, and valued, even if they're sharing something that might be difficult to hear or understand. This creates a space of safety and respect where both of you can show up as your true selves without judgment.

Embracing Vulnerability as a Path to Deeper Love

The power of vulnerability lies in its ability to create genuine, lasting bonds. When both of you are willing to be open—without fear of rejection or judgment—you create a relationship that feels secure, supportive, and grounded in trust. Vulnerability then becomes the bridge that not only connects you but also strengthens you, helping you both feel more resilient in the face of life's challenges.

In embracing vulnerability, you're not only building a healthier relationship but also allowing yourself to experience love in its most authentic, freeing form. This may feel a bit uncomfortable at first, but as you lean into this openness, you'll find a level of connection that's deeper than you may have thought possible—one that's built on a foundation of honesty, respect, and true emotional intimacy.

CHAPTER 12: CREATING A SECURE LOVE FOUNDATION

Create and sustain love

Creating and sustaining a secure, lasting love might sound like a lofty goal, but it's truly within reach—and it doesn't require anything extraordinary, just consistent effort, trust, and the right mindset. A secure love foundation isn't about finding the perfect partner or achieving some ideal relationship. It's about building a partnership rooted in mutual respect, understanding, and genuine commitment to each other's well-being.

1. Laying the Foundation of Trust

Trust is the bedrock of any secure relationship. When you and your partner can count on each other—whether it's keeping promises, supporting each other through tough times, or being emotionally present—it builds a sense of safety that's essential for long-lasting love. To create this trust, start by being clear about your intentions, showing consistency in your actions, and always aiming to be open and honest. *It's okay if it takes time*; trust grows gradually as you both experience each other's reliability.

2. Nurturing Emotional Security Daily

Secure love thrives when both partners feel emotionally safe, able to be their authentic selves without fear of judgment or rejection. This means checking in regularly, sharing your feelings, and listening actively. Practice being open about what you need and encouraging your partner to do the same. Even small gestures, like a thoughtful text or taking a few minutes to connect at the end of the day, can reinforce the emotional bond between you.

3. Prioritizing Each Other's Growth

In a secure relationship, both partners support each other's personal growth. This means respecting each other's goals, dreams, and aspirations, even when they don't directly involve the relationship. When you encourage your partner to pursue what makes them happy or fulfilled, you're creating a foundation that values individuality as well as togetherness. In turn, this strengthens the bond, as each of you feels respected and supported.

4. Communicating Through the Ups and Downs

No relationship is perfect. There will be challenges, misunderstandings, and maybe even periods of doubt. What matters most is how you handle these moments together. Instead of letting emotions build up, address issues openly and kindly. Express how you feel and actively listen to your partner's perspective without jumping to conclusions. Approaching conflicts with patience and empathy builds resilience, showing each other that no problem is bigger than the commitment you share.

5. Reinforcing Love with Small Acts of Kindness

Sometimes, the little things carry the most weight. Acts of kindness—whether it's preparing a favorite meal, sharing a heartfelt compliment, or showing appreciation for your partner's efforts—create an environment of care and affection. These gestures remind each other that you're valued, loved, and respected, reinforcing the foundation of security you're building together.

6. Staying Open to Growth as a Couple

Lastly, building secure, long-lasting love means understanding that relationships evolve. Your needs may change, as might your partner's, and it's essential to remain open to adapting together. Celebrate each other's successes, support each other through setbacks, and find ways to refresh and deepen your connection over time. This keeps the relationship dynamic, alive, and ready to meet new challenges.

Embracing the Journey of Secure Love

Creating a secure, lasting love isn't a one-time achievement; it's a journey you embark on together, with both of you showing up consistently to make each other feel safe, cherished, and valued. As you both commit to these small yet powerful acts, you're building a love that's resilient, joyful, and ready to stand the test of time. You'll find that the more you nurture this foundation, the stronger and more secure your relationship becomes, bringing you closer to the fulfilling, lasting love you both deserve.

Reinforcing emotional security

Long-term emotional security is like the heart of a healthy relationship—it beats consistently, sustaining both partners through ups, downs, and everything in between. Developing practices that reinforce emotional security isn't about perfection but about showing up daily with intention and care. Here's how you can cultivate emotional security in your relationship, year after year.

1. Keep Communication Honest and Open

One of the best ways to maintain emotional security over time is by fostering a habit of open communication. Make it a point to talk about your feelings, your worries, and even your insecurities. When something's on your mind, bring it up gently and listen without jumping to conclusions when your partner does the same. Over time, these honest conversations build a shared understanding, a "safe space" where both of you feel free to be your real selves, knowing you won't face judgment or criticism.

2. Stay Consistent with Small Acts of Care

We often think big gestures make the difference, but it's actually the small, consistent acts of kindness that mean the most. These could be as simple as a warm greeting after work, an encouraging word before a big day, or an unexpected "thank you" for something small. By keeping up these thoughtful habits, you create an environment that feels supportive, showing each other that love and appreciation are woven into your everyday lives.

3. Prioritize Quality Time Together

Life gets busy, and it's easy to take time together for granted. Make it a priority to spend regular quality time with your partner—without distractions. This could be through weekly date nights, shared hobbies, or even a simple walk where you're focused on each other. When you carve out this space, it sends a powerful message that the relationship matters to you and that you're committed to nurturing it.

4. Validate Each Other's Feelings Regularly

Validation is one of the simplest yet most powerful ways to reinforce emotional security. Acknowledge your partner's feelings, even if you may not always fully understand them. Sometimes just saying, "I see why you feel that way" or "I'm here for you, no matter what" can mean the world. By affirming each other's emotions, you create an environment of acceptance, letting each other know that your feelings are respected and understood.

5. Celebrate the Good Times—and Reflect on Them Often

In a secure relationship, it's easy to get caught up in "solving" issues and focusing on areas of growth. But equally important is the joy of celebrating good times together. Whether it's a big achievement or a little milestone, take time to recognize these moments. And don't be afraid to reminisce on these memories from time to time—it reinforces the positive foundation you've built and reminds both of you of all the wonderful experiences you've shared.

6. Revisit Your Shared Goals and Vision Regularly

Over time, your individual goals and dreams can shift, which is completely natural. Periodically checking in with each other about your shared vision—what you both want for the future and how you see your lives together—can provide reassurance and deepen your bond. This practice keeps you aligned and helps ensure that your relationship remains a space where both of you feel supported in moving forward together.

7. Practice Forgiveness and Patience

No one is perfect, and mistakes are inevitable. But emotional security thrives when both partners show patience and extend forgiveness when things go wrong. When misunderstandings happen, or when one of you makes a mistake, it's the act of listening, understanding, and letting go of resentment that keeps the relationship strong. By doing this, you both create a foundation of acceptance, knowing you can be human together without fear of abandonment.

Long-Term Security as a Shared Journey

Practices like these, when kept up over time, reinforce the secure foundation you've built together. They remind you both that your relationship is a haven—a place where you can always come back to for safety, understanding, and love. Emotional security isn't about never having challenges; it's about knowing that no matter what life throws your way, you'll face it together, stronger with each passing day.

When setbacks occur?

Setbacks are inevitable in any relationship. They might come as misunderstandings, moments of insecurity, or external challenges that shake the foundation you've been carefully building. But here's the thing: setbacks don't define the strength of your relationship—how you handle them does. Knowing how to stay grounded in security, even when things feel shaky, can make all the difference in keeping your bond strong and moving forward together.

1. Pause and Breathe: Don't React in the Heat of the Moment

In moments of conflict or disappointment, emotions can run high. It's tempting to react immediately, but often our first response is driven by old fears or defensive instincts. Take a moment to pause, breathe, and create a little space between the trigger and your reaction. Remind yourself that you're safe, and that a quick reaction might not align with your long-term goals. This small moment can help you respond with thoughtfulness rather than defensiveness.

2. Acknowledge the Setback Without Self-Blame

When a setback happens, it's easy to fall into the trap of self-blame—thinking that it happened because you're not "good enough" or that it's somehow your fault. Instead, acknowledge that challenges are a natural part of any relationship. Remember, being secure doesn't mean never facing difficulties; it means learning how to handle them with resilience. Give yourself credit for the progress you've made and trust that this setback is just another stepping stone.

3. Communicate Calmly and Honestly

Once emotions settle, create a space to communicate openly about the setback. Share your perspective honestly, focusing on how you feel rather than placing blame. Let your partner know that you're committed to finding a solution together, reinforcing that both of you are on the same team. These conversations, even if difficult, help rebuild trust and remind both of you that setbacks are opportunities to strengthen your relationship, not weaken it.

4. Revisit Your Shared Goals and Values

Setbacks are often easier to navigate when you remember the bigger picture. Take some time to reflect on the values and goals you both share. Why did you start this journey together in the first place? What vision do you have for your future? Regrounding yourselves in these shared commitments can help remind you that this is a small moment in a much larger story—a story of growth, support, and mutual love.

5. Offer Reassurance to Each Other

In the face of setbacks, we often need extra reassurance, and that's okay. Tell each other that this rough patch doesn't change your feelings or commitment. Simple words like, "We'll get through this" or "I'm here for you" can go a long way in making both of you feel safe and secure. Reassuring each other is not about ignoring the issue but about acknowledging that even in challenging times, your bond remains solid.

6. Treat the Setback as a Learning Opportunity

Each setback carries a lesson. Maybe it reveals an area where communication could be improved or shows an old wound that still needs healing. Look at this moment as a chance to learn something valuable about yourselves or your relationship. This reframing allows you to treat setbacks not as failures but as opportunities for growth. You'll often find that coming through a difficult time together brings you even closer.

7. Recommit to Practicing Self-Care and Boundaries

Setbacks can sometimes leave us feeling emotionally depleted, so it's essential to take care of yourself. Recommit to self-care practices that help you feel balanced and at peace, whether it's spending time with friends, engaging in a hobby, or simply taking time for yourself. Remember that secure relationships thrive when both individuals maintain a sense of wholeness and self-worth, even when times get tough.

Resilience Through Setbacks: A Shared Journey

Setbacks are a reminder that building a secure, loving relationship is a journey, not a destination. Each step, including the missteps, is part of growing and strengthening together. By staying grounded, communicating openly, and reminding each other of your shared foundation, you not only navigate these setbacks but come through them with an even stronger connection.

In the end, setbacks don't have to be setbacks at all—they're opportunities to recommit, deepen your trust, and show each other that, no matter what, you're in this together. And that's what makes a relationship truly secure: the knowledge that, together, you can face anything that comes your way.

PART 5: YOUR 12-WEEK JOURNEY TO SECURE ATTACHMENT

CHAPTER 13: WEEK-BY-WEEK ACTION PLAN

We're diving into a hands-on, week-by-week action plan to guide you through the transformative journey to secure attachment. Here, we'll walk through each week's focus, so you have a clear, practical roadmap for building the confidence, trust, and security you need to thrive in your relationships.

A Breakdown of Key Milestones for Each Week

Over the next 12 weeks, think of each week as a small, intentional step forward. Rather than expecting drastic overnight change, we'll focus on gradual shifts that build upon one another, allowing you to internalize new habits and ways of thinking.

Week 1: Understanding Your Starting Point

We'll start by examining your attachment style in depth and the specific patterns that may have been holding you back. This week is about awareness—observing yourself without judgment, so you can set clear, realistic intentions for this journey.

Week 2: Recognizing Fear-Based Behaviors

In Week 2, we'll delve into the roots of your fear-driven reactions. You'll start identifying the moments when insecurity, jealousy, or anxiety surfaces and learn to recognize these as natural responses, not unchangeable traits.

Week 3: Thought-Stopping Techniques

This week, we'll focus on practical tools for managing negative thought spirals. You'll learn thought-stopping techniques that help you intercept anxious thoughts before they take over, allowing you to refocus and regain control.

Week 4: Practicing Self-Compassion

Secure attachment begins with treating yourself kindly. This week, we'll work on building self-compassion through exercises designed to help you forgive yourself, celebrate your progress, and show up with more understanding in relationships.

Week 5: Setting Personal Boundaries

Here, we'll go deeper into establishing healthy boundaries—what they look like, how to set them, and why they're essential for emotional security. Practicing boundaries helps you feel safe and respected in all interactions.

Week 6: Communicating Your Needs

Communication is key, especially when it comes to needs and expectations. This week, we'll practice expressing what you need in relationships clearly and assertively, without fear or guilt, so you feel empowered and heard.

Week 7: Cultivating Mindfulness in Relationships

Mindfulness helps you stay present, even in moments of anxiety or stress. This week, you'll learn mindfulness techniques to reduce reactivity and increase your capacity to respond calmly, helping you feel more grounded in relationships.

Week 8: Building Trust Through Small Steps

Trust grows through consistent, small actions over time. This week, you'll explore ways to gradually build trust with your partner by fostering transparency, honesty, and reliability.

Week 9: Reinforcing Emotional Resilience

This week reinforces your capacity to stay strong and secure, even when things don't go perfectly.

Week 10: Developing a Secure Sense of Self-Worth

This week, we'll focus on separating your self-worth from others' opinions and actions. By affirming your inherent value, you'll cultivate a stable sense of confidence that's independent of any relationship.

Week 11: Deepening Emotional Intimacy

With a secure foundation in place, this week is about opening up and sharing deeper aspects of yourself with your partner. Vulnerability fosters closeness and trust, helping you build a more profound emotional connection.

Week 12: Reflecting, Celebrating, and Looking Ahead

In our final week, we'll reflect on your progress, celebrate your growth, and set intentions for maintaining your new, secure attachment style. You'll look forward with confidence, knowing you have the tools and resilience to navigate relationships with grace and self-assurance.

This 12-week journey is about empowering you to make gradual, sustainable changes that lead to lasting security. By taking it one week at a time, you'll feel a genuine shift as you move from anxious patterns toward a life filled with stable, loving connections.

Weekly challenges

To make this 12-week journey even more engaging and impactful, each week will include a set of challenges to help you practice and reflect on what you're learning. These challenges are designed to build confidence step-by-step and give you tangible ways to see your progress as you work toward secure attachment.

Weekly Challenges to Practice and Reflect on Attachment Growth

Each week, we'll provide you with a simple but meaningful challenge tailored to the theme of that week. These are small, actionable steps that reinforce your growth, with moments of reflection to keep you mindful and motivated.

Week 1: Self-Observation Challenge

Challenge: Throughout the week, notice moments when you feel anxious or uncertain in interactions. Write down five (7) triggers and how you reacted.

   1. **Trigger**

____

____

____

____

Your reaction

____

____

____

____

2. Trigger

____

____

____

____

Your reaction

____

____

____

____

3. Trigger

____

____

____

____

Your reaction

____

____

____

____

____

4. Trigger

____

____

____

Your reaction

____

____

____

5. Trigger

____

____

____

Your reaction

____

____

____

6. Trigger

____

____

____

____

Your reaction

____

____

____

____

7. Trigger

____

____

____

____

Your reaction

____

____

____

____

Reflection: At the end of the week, look back at your notes and notice any common themes. This will give you insight into your patterns and prepare you to start shifting them.

Week 2: Facing Fears Journal Exercise

Challenge: Identify one fear-driven thought each day and write it down. Then, challenge yourself to respond to this thought as if you were comforting a friend, using supportive language. Write down seven (7) fear driven thoughts and your responses.

1. Thought

____

____

____

____

Your respnse using supportive language

____

____

____

____

2. Thought

____

____

____

____

Your respnse using supportive language

____

____

____

____

____

3. Thought

____

____

____

____

Your respnse using supportive language

____

____

____

____

4. Thought

____

____

____

Your respnse using supportive language

____

____

____

____

5. Thought

Your respnse using supportive language

6. Thought

Your respnse using supportive language

7. Thought

____

____

Your respnse using supportive language
____

____

____

____

Reflection: By re-reading your journal entries, notice how it feels to replace fear with compassion. This is your first step toward breaking the hold of fear-based thinking.

Week 3: Thought-Interruption Practice

Challenge: When you catch yourself in a negative thought spiral, interrupt it with a physical action—stand up, stretch, or take a deep breath. Replace the thought with a simple, grounding affirmation like "I am secure." Write down seven (7) negative thoughts and the physical actions you interrupted them with.

1. Negative thought
____

____

____

____

Physical action

2. Negative thought

Physical action

3. Negative thought

Physical action

4. Negative thought

Physical action

5. Negative thought

Physical action

6. Negative thought

Physical action

____

____

____

7.   Negative thought

____

____

____

Physical action

____

____

____

Reflection: Reflect on how these interruptions impacted your emotional state and sense of control. Notice any shift in your confidence and mental clarity.

Week 4: Self-Compassion Challenge

Challenge: Each day, make a list of three small ways you practiced kindness toward yourself. This could be anything from giving yourself a break to letting go of a harsh judgment. Write down three small ways you were kind to yourself each day for 7 days.

DAY 1

1.

2.

3.

DAY 2

1.

2.

3.

DAY 3

1.

2.

3.

DAY 4

1.

2.

3.

DAY 5

1.

2.

3.

DAY 6

1.

2.

3.

DAY 7

1.

____

2. ____

____

3. ____

____

____

Reflection: At week's end, review your list and take pride in these acts of self-compassion. This exercise will help you see self-care as a crucial part of feeling secure.

Week 5: Personal Boundaries Inventory

Challenge: Think about one boundary you'd like to set, either at work, with family, or in your relationship. Practice communicating this boundary clearly, even if it's just a gentle reminder to yourself. Write down boundaries you'll like to set.

____

____

____

____

____

____

Reflection: Reflect on how establishing this boundary made you feel. Did it bring relief, comfort, or confidence? Boundaries are foundational to feeling safe and respected.

Week 6: Needs Communication Exercise

Challenge: Identify your personal needs you want to share with a partner or friend this week. Practice saying it out loud in a clear, positive way, even if it's in a low-stakes context. Write down 7 personal needs.

1. My Personal Need

2. My Personal Need

3. My Personal Need

4. My Personal Need

____

____

____

5. My Personal Need

____

____

____

6. My Personal Need

____

____

____

7. My Personal Need

____

____

____

Reflection: After expressing your need, take note of your emotional response. Did you feel relief, pride, or hesitation? This practice builds confidence in advocating for yourself.

Week 7: Mindfulness Practice

Challenge: Set aside five minutes each day to practice mindful breathing. Focus on each breath and gently bring your thoughts back whenever they wander. Write down how you feel each day after this mindful breathing exercise.

I feel ____

____

____

I feel ____

____

____

I feel ____

____

____

I feel ____

____

____

I feel ____

____

____

I feel _______________________________________

____

____

I feel _______________________________________

____

____

Reflection: Reflect on any emotional shifts after practicing mindfulness. Notice if you felt calmer, less reactive, or more present with yourself and others.

Week 8: Trust-Building Action

Challenge: Commit to one small act this week that builds trust with someone close—keeping a promise, being on time, or simply following through on something you said you'd do. Write down the act you've commited to.

I have commited to _______________________________________

____

____

Reflection: Reflect on the impact of this action. Recognize that trust is a gift you both give and receive, one small step at a time.

Week 9: Emotional Resilience Check-In

Challenge: Set aside a few minutes each day to check in with yourself. Ask, "What do I need right now?" and honor whatever answer comes up, whether it's rest, joy, or reflection. Do this for 7 days, write down your needs and how you honored them.

1. What I need right now?

____

____

____

____

I honored my need by ____

____

____

2. What I need right now?

____

____

____

I honored my need by ____

3. What I need right now?

____

____

____

I honored my need by _______________________________

____

____

4. What I need right now?

____

____

____

I honored my need by _______________________________

____

____

5. What I need right now?

____

____

____

____

I honored my need by ___________________________

____

____

6. What I need right now?

____

____

____

I honored my need by ___________________________

____

____

7. What I need right now?

____

____

____

I honored my need by ___________________________

____

____

Reflection: Reflect on how these moments of self-care reinforced your resilience and strength, giving you the emotional security to handle challenges with more ease.

Week 10: Self-Worth Affirmation Practice

Challenge: Each day, say one affirmation that reinforces your self-worth, like "I am deserving of love" or "I am enough as I am."

I am ____

____

____

I am ____

____

____

I am ____

____

____

I am ____

____

____

I am ____

____

____

I am ____

____

____

I am ____

____

____

Reflection: Take note of any shifts in your confidence over the week. Small affirmations can help anchor your sense of worth independent of others' opinions.

Week 11: Vulnerability Challenge

Challenge: Open up to someone you trust about something meaningful to you. This could be a hope, a fear, or a personal value—anything that feels like a deeper part of you. Write down what you told the person and how it made you feel.

What did you open up about?

____

How did you feel about opening up to someone you trust?

Reflection: Reflect on how vulnerability felt. Did it strengthen your connection with the person? Recognize that sharing authentically can foster security and trust.

Week 12: Celebrate Your Growth

Challenge: Take time to reflect on one area where you've seen the most growth in yourself over the past 12 weeks. Write down how you've changed and any new goals you want to set.

What area have you experienced growth?

____

____

____

How much have you changed?

____

____

____

What new goals do you want to set?

____

____

____

Reflection: Celebrate your journey! Recognize the growth, resilience, and strength you've gained, and let this moment anchor your commitment to a secure and fulfilling future.

These weekly challenges are designed to be manageable yet impactful, encouraging you to practice and reflect in real, meaningful ways. You'll find yourself naturally shifting from anxious habits toward more confident, secure, and loving ways of connecting. Remember, this journey is about progress, not perfection, and every small step counts.

CHAPTER 14: MAINTAINING YOUR EMOTIONAL GROWTH

After completing this 12-week journey, you've come so far in building secure attachment, self-compassion, and emotional resilience. But just like any other area of growth, maintaining your progress will take ongoing care and attention. The good news? You already have the tools. Now it's about keeping those tools within reach, using them when needed, and trusting that you have what it takes to keep growing.

How to Stay on the Path

1. Reflect Regularly on Your Progress

Set aside a little time each month to check in with yourself. Reflect on the small and large steps you've taken, the challenges you've overcome, and the changes you've noticed. It could be as simple as journaling a few lines about how you handled a difficult interaction or felt more secure in a relationship. By acknowledging your growth, you'll keep your progress alive and stay motivated to continue.

2. Keep Using Your Favorite Techniques

Throughout the 12 weeks, you tried out different exercises, practices, and tools. Some of them might have felt transformative, while others might not have resonated as much. Focus on the techniques that genuinely helped you feel secure and grounded. Whether it's mindfulness, cognitive restructuring, setting boundaries, or self-compassion practices, keep these tools in your back pocket and use them as needed.

3. Stay Aware of Old Patterns

It's natural to sometimes feel yourself slipping back into older patterns—everyone does. When you notice these feelings or behaviors, don't be discouraged. Instead, see them as opportunities to pause and reflect. Why might this old pattern be coming up again? Could it be a reaction to stress, change, or uncertainty? Acknowledging these moments with curiosity rather than judgment will help you manage them without getting overwhelmed.

4. Stay Connected with Supportive People

Supportive relationships—whether friends, family, a partner, or a therapist—are incredibly valuable. They remind you of your worth, offer encouragement, and reinforce your secure attachment goals. Lean on these people, especially during tough times, and continue to build trust and openness with them. Don't hesitate to reach out for support when you need it; you don't have to handle everything alone.

5. Remind Yourself That Growth Isn't Linear

There will be times when you feel like you're on top of your secure attachment journey, and other times when old insecurities might resurface. This doesn't mean you're moving backward; it's a natural part of personal growth. Remember, the goal isn't perfection; it's progress and self-awareness. Be kind to yourself during setbacks, and trust that each challenge brings a new opportunity to strengthen your skills.

6. Celebrate the Wins—Big and Small

Don't wait for major milestones to celebrate your progress. Every time you set a boundary, ask for what you need, or choose not to engage in a negative spiral, that's worth acknowledging. Celebrating these small victories reinforces your commitment to secure attachment and reminds you of how far you've come.

This journey is about building a secure, confident foundation for yourself and your relationships, and you're already well on your way. By staying connected to these practices, revisiting your favorite techniques, and giving yourself grace in moments of challenge, you'll be able to keep this foundation strong. Remember:

you have everything you need to stay on this path. Trust in your resilience and know that the secure attachment you've built is here to stay.

Building support systems

We all need people in our corner who remind us of our worth, who hold us accountable to our goals, and who provide comfort when things get tough. Having a strong support network doesn't mean you're dependent on others for happiness or security; instead, it means you're creating a safe, interconnected environment that nurtures your growth.

Building Support Systems for Long-Term Emotional Resilience

1. Identify Your Inner Circle

Think about the people in your life who truly understand you. Who are those friends, family members, or mentors you can trust with your struggles, victories, and vulnerabilities? They don't have to be many, but they should be people who make you feel safe and accepted. Reach out to them, let them know how important their support is, and give yourself permission to lean on them when you need it. True friends want to be there for you, and nurturing these bonds will deepen your sense of belonging and emotional security.

2. Set Boundaries and Expectations with Loved Ones

Part of building a supportive network is openly communicating your needs. Be clear with those around you about the type of support you find most helpful. Do you prefer words of affirmation, a listening ear, or gentle reminders to stay focused on your goals? Setting these expectations can make a big difference in feeling supported and understood, and it empowers your loved ones to show up in ways that feel genuinely helpful to you.

3. Seek Like-Minded Communities

Sometimes, connecting with others who have similar experiences or goals can be incredibly reinforcing. Look for support groups, workshops, or online communities that focus on emotional resilience, attachment work, or personal growth. Whether it's in person or virtual, having a space to share your journey with people who "get it" can be comforting and motivating.

4. Don't Be Afraid to Ask for Help

It's okay to need a little extra guidance sometimes. Whether through therapy, coaching, or even a trusted friend, asking for help when you're feeling stuck or overwhelmed can be transformative. Therapists and counselors, especially those experienced with attachment issues, can provide tailored support and offer new tools to help you stay resilient. And remember, asking for help is not a sign of weakness—it's a powerful step toward self-care and long-term well-being.

5. Give Back to Your Support System

Support is a two-way street. By showing up for others, you reinforce a network that's there for everyone involved. Be a listening ear, offer empathy, and celebrate the people in your life as they pursue their goals. The more we nurture our relationships by giving back, the stronger those bonds become—and these connections will sustain both you and your loved ones through the ups and downs of life.

6. Practice Vulnerability

Opening up to others can feel scary, especially when we're used to guarding our emotions. But building lasting connections means allowing people to see us fully—the good, the challenging, the real. Vulnerability strengthens bonds and helps others feel closer to us. In safe and trusted spaces, try sharing a bit more of your journey, your dreams, or your insecurities. The warmth and support you receive in return can be a powerful reminder of why building these connections matters.

Creating and maintaining support systems is a powerful way to build long-term resilience and secure attachment. You're never alone on this journey—remember that there are people who want to see you thrive, and they're ready to stand by you every step of the way.

Cognitive-behavioral tools

The beauty of these tools is that they're designed to help you work through emotional roadblocks by reshaping your thoughts, challenging unhelpful beliefs, and grounding yourself in healthier perspectives.

Continuing to Use Cognitive-Behavioral Tools for Future Relationship Challenges

When we face conflicts, insecurities, or times of uncertainty in our relationships, it's easy for old habits to sneak back in. But using cognitive-behavioral techniques can help you pause, assess the situation, and respond in a way that aligns with your secure self.

1. Recognizing Negative Thought Patterns

One of the first steps in handling any challenge is identifying the negative thought patterns that may be triggering it. These can include jumping to conclusions, catastrophizing (assuming the worst will happen), or interpreting your partner's actions in a way that fuels insecurity. By recognizing these thoughts, you can then question their accuracy. For instance, instead of assuming that your partner's busy day is a sign they're withdrawing from you, consider alternative explanations—maybe they're just genuinely tired or distracted.

2. Thought-Stopping Techniques to Calm Your Mind

In moments of anxiety or stress, thought-stopping exercises can be a lifesaver. These methods help interrupt negative spirals before they gain too much momentum. A simple "Stop" command, a deep breath, or a brief focus on something around you—like the feel of the chair beneath you or a sound in the room—can bring you back to the present. Practicing this technique reinforces your control over your reactions and calms any anxiety that might arise from relationship worries.

3. Reframing to Build Healthier Beliefs

Cognitive reframing is all about taking a situation that feels negative and finding a more balanced, constructive view. For example, if you find yourself thinking, "I'm not good enough," try reframing it with evidence to the contrary, such as, "I bring a lot of value to this relationship, and I am worthy of love." This exercise builds resilience by helping you see your relationships—and yourself—from a more secure, positive perspective.

4. Using Problem-Solving Techniques Together

When challenges do come up with your partner, consider using the same cognitive-behavioral methods you've practiced to work through them together. Instead of viewing the conflict as something divisive, approach it as a team. Communicate openly about what you each feel, brainstorm solutions, and look for compromises that honor both of your needs. This builds trust and shows both of you that challenges can be a stepping stone for growth, not a threat to your bond.

5. Reflection and Self-Assessment

Make time to reflect on the way you're using these tools and how they're impacting your relationships. This could mean journaling about a recent interaction, noting what thoughts and beliefs surfaced, and considering how well the tools worked. Self-assessment keeps you aligned with your secure attachment goals and lets you see the progress you're making.

These tools will be valuable companions on your journey. Every time you use them, you reinforce healthier habits that not only deepen your relationships but also strengthen the connection you have with yourself. By continuing to lean on these strategies, you're equipping yourself to face whatever relationship challenges come your way with confidence, calm, and a secure sense of self.

CONCLUSION

The work you've done has been more than just learning new skills; it's been a transformation in how you see yourself, your relationships, and the life you're creating.

Recap of Key Lessons

1. Understanding and Accepting Your Attachment Style

In the beginning, we delved into the origins of anxious attachment and how early relationships shaped the way you experience closeness and connection. This understanding laid the groundwork for everything else, helping you see that attachment isn't fixed—it's something you can shape and heal.

2. Moving Beyond Fear of Abandonment

You worked on breaking free from that persistent fear of rejection and abandonment. You learned how fear fuels jealousy, insecurity, and anxiety and practiced ways to recognize when it was creeping into your behavior. By breaking down these patterns, you took huge steps toward feeling safer and more secure, both within yourself and with others.

3. Managing Relationship Anxiety and Building Self-Worth

We explored strategies to manage anxiety with cognitive-behavioral tools, thought-stopping techniques, and mindfulness practices. You've seen how important it is to detach your self-worth from relationship outcomes, learning instead to ground it in who you are. This is one of the most empowering changes you've made, as it strengthens your core and brings you closer to a secure sense of self.

4. Setting Boundaries and Asserting Needs

Throughout the journey, you've also been practicing setting boundaries—not as walls, but as healthy expressions of what you need to feel safe and respected. This skill is so powerful because it allows you to communicate openly and maintain emotional safety without compromising your identity. You learned that boundaries aren't selfish; they're essential for your well-being and, ultimately, for the health of your relationships.

5. Rewiring Your Attachment Patterns and Building Emotional Resilience

By moving away from fear-driven reactions, you've started responding to situations with calm and confidence. You also practiced exercises to shift unhelpful beliefs and reframe your thoughts, reinforcing your growth. The work you've done here builds emotional resilience, a trait that will stay with you well beyond these pages.

6. Fostering Trust and Creating Secure Bonds

The final weeks guided you in fostering trust and nurturing emotional intimacy. You discovered that true intimacy grows from vulnerability and authenticity, not from trying to avoid conflict or insecurity. Now, you have strategies to deepen connections and navigate challenges with love, trust, and self-assurance.

Where You Stand Today

Every chapter, every exercise, and every reflection brought you closer to the secure attachment you deserve. You're no longer held back by the old, automatic fears and reactions that once shaped your interactions. Instead, you're embracing relationships from a place of wholeness, with a toolkit for handling whatever comes your way.

This isn't the end of your journey; it's just the beginning of a life filled with more secure, loving connections. Remember, your progress may sometimes feel gradual, but each step you've taken is a lasting one. As you move forward, keep these lessons close and trust in the growth you've achieved. You've built a foundation of security, love, and self-worth that will support you for a lifetime.

Live confidently and securely

After all the growth you've experienced, you're ready to let go of the worry and doubt that anxious attachment once brought. You now have the tools, insights, and most importantly, the belief in yourself to truly feel secure.

Living Confidently in Your Relationships

Living confidently means you trust yourself. You've done the hard work of understanding and healing, and now you know your worth isn't dependent on anyone else. You're grounded in who you are, and that makes a world of difference. When you communicate, it's no longer from a place of fear or neediness but from a place of strength and clarity. You're no longer asking for love or acceptance—you're bringing your whole, worthy self into every interaction, knowing you deserve respect and kindness in return.

Confidence also means being able to accept vulnerability without feeling overwhelmed. You've learned that being open doesn't mean losing control; instead, it's how true connection happens. By allowing yourself to be seen, imperfections and all, you invite the same authenticity from others. And when conflicts arise, as they will, you can handle them calmly, knowing that one moment doesn't define your worth or your relationship. This self-assurance means you can be honest, even in hard conversations, without fear of abandonment.

Building a Secure Foundation in Each Relationship

Security, as you've seen, isn't just a destination—it's a way of being. It's knowing that whatever happens, you have the ability to manage it. You've set boundaries, you know your needs, and you're not afraid to ask for them to be met. By keeping these values in focus, you create a stable foundation for your relationships to thrive. The security you've built allows you to lean into relationships, trusting that you can weather ups and downs with resilience.

Living securely also means embracing the journey rather than always trying to predict or control the outcome. Relationships will always bring challenges, but now you have the emotional tools to face those with grace. You can lean into love without losing yourself, enjoy closeness without clinging, and trust without needing constant reassurance. When you feel moments of insecurity arise, you can recognize them as just that—moments, not truths— and use the techniques you've learned to find your center again.

Moving Forward with Strength and Security

You're walking into your future from a place of empowerment. You're no longer defined by anxious patterns or reactions. Instead, you're choosing each day to live with confidence, to stay grounded in security, and to open your heart to love in a healthy, balanced way. Remember, secure attachment isn't about perfection—it's about progress, resilience, and a deep belief in your own worth.

You've earned this confidence, this security, and this new chapter of love and happiness. And it's just the beginning.

www.ingramcontent.com/pod-product-compliance
Lightning Source LLC
Chambersburg PA
CBHW051559250726
48653CB00004BA/1227